Family
Party
Games

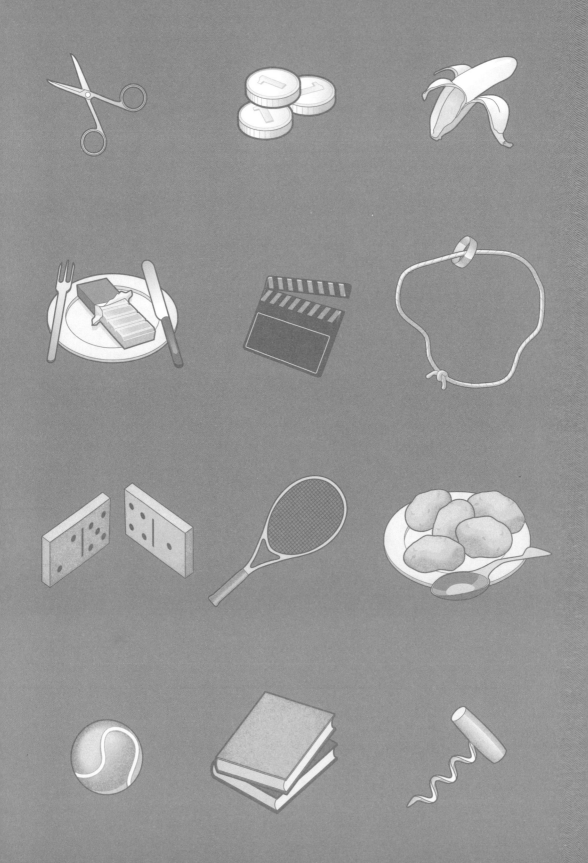

hamlyn

Family Party Games

100 fun games for all occasions

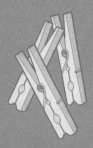

Peter Arnold

First published in Great Britain in 2005 by
Hamlyn, an imprint of Octopus Publishing Group Ltd
2–4 Heron Quays, London E14 4JP

Distributed in the United States and Canada by
Sterling Publishing Co., Inc.
387 Park Avenue South, New York, NY 10016-8810

ISBN 0 600 61271 6
EAN 9780600612711

A CIP catalogue record for this book is available from
the British Library

Printed and bound in China

10 9 8 7 6 5 4 3 2 1

The publisher cannot accept any legal responsibility or
liability for any injury or accident resulting from playing
these games.

Contents

Introduction

Everybody loves a party. The habit usually starts at school, when classmates invite each other to their parties, and the peculiar excitement of being invited to a party, or inviting friends to yours, remains all through life. Perhaps the best parties of all are the family parties, which bring many age groups together at times like birthdays and Christmas.

The secret of hosting a good family party is to provide enough activities to keep everybody from the toddlers to grandad entertained. A big help is clearly a stock of games designed to

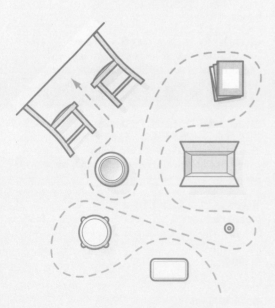

keep the very young happy until bedtime and then divert the teenagers and adults who remain in the evening. This book is designed to give the party host enough ideas to ensure that there are no slack periods during the day and that everybody joins in and has a chance to play.

The book is divided for convenience into twelve rather loose sections: games for young children; musical games; racing games; hunting games; guessing games; parties for all ages; games in the garden; travel games; pencil and paper games; quick-to-learn card games; dice and domino games and games for the older generation. These categories overlap, of course. Most indoor games could, on a fine day, be played in the garden, and some travel games, suggested for keeping children happy on car journeys, do not necessarily have to be played in the car, so it is hoped that potential party-givers will go through the whole book and choose which games would be most suitable for their intended guests.

In choosing games we have omitted some categories, like singing games for the young, since these are mostly learned at school or from television. Apart from that, we have included some old and tried favourites like Musical chairs, but hope there will be many games the reader will find new and worth trying.

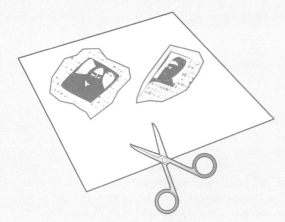

Occasionally we have attached a warning box to a game, pointing out that care must be taken to avoid damage either to your property and belongings or to the participants. Most of these are fairly obvious, but it is as well when throwing a party to remember that, especially when youngsters are dashing about, or there is water present, there is always a possibility of accidents and you should try to anticipate the potential for accidents and prevent them.

But gloomy notes should not impinge on a party, so have a good one!

Each game itemizes at the top of the page the age range for which it is considered suitable, the number of players who can take part, what sort of occasion it is best for, and what objects you will need. We have not suggested anything elaborate in the way of props, but where a little advance preparation would improve a game we have set this out in an introductory paragraph or two.

We have concentrated only on games, and not on the other trappings of a party, such as decorations, balloons etc., of which the host will know best what is suitable. Nor have we suggested prizes for games, although with small children little prizes add to the excitement. But they can lead to disappointment among the losers, too, so should be trivial in nature.

Hunt the thimble

Age range 3+
Number of players Any
Ideal for Parties of young children who need a simple game to occupy them
What you will need A small object, traditionally a thimble

This is a very simple game which, nevertheless, needs to be supervised by an adult or two, especially when very young children are involved, since even some three-year-olds have not yet grasped the principle of hiding things. Traditionally, the object to be hidden is a thimble, but any other small, distinctive object such as a brightly coloured button or a cork from a wine bottle will suffice.

How to play
There are two ways to play the game.
1. One child is chosen to be first to hide the thimble. The other children leave the room while she hides it. When the thimble is hidden, the other children come into the room and wander about trying to find the thimble. The first to succeed then has the privilege of hiding the thimble for the next game.

2. One child is chosen to go out of the room while one of the remaining children who stay in the room hides the thimble. The seeker is then let in to search. If she starts a long way from the thimble the children call out that she's 'cold', as she approaches it they call 'getting warmer', and so on through 'warm', 'hot', 'very hot' and 'boiling' until she actually finds it. The finder then has the role of hiding the thimble while the next seeker leaves the room.

> ❗ **WARNING**
> Tell the children – and ensure that it is true – that the thimble is always 'hidden' where it can be seen, so there is no need to open drawers or cupboards or look underneath ornaments. You do not want any breakages!

Age range 3+
Number of players 4–7
Ideal for Entertaining young children
What you will need A large house with, ideally, many places to hide

Sardines

This is a hiding game which will need two or three adults to supervise as it entails children wandering at will around your house.

How to play

In this game a certain amount of darkness adds to the pleasure, but the age and disposition of the children will decide how much darkness you think will be desirable.

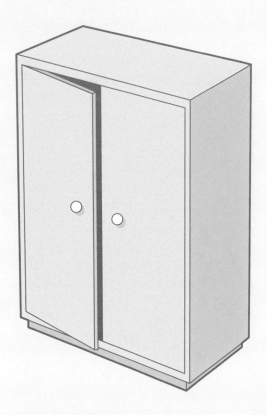

One child is chosen to be the 'sardine' and to go away and hide while the other children are kept in a separate room. The sardine must hide in a space where other children can join him, such as under a bed, in a large cupboard or under the stairs. For this reason, it is best for an adult to help find the hiding place.

When the sardine is safely hidden, the other children are let loose to find him. Adults should encourage them to split up and go their separate ways all over the house.

When a seeker finds the sardine, she joins the sardine in the hiding place, and gradually the hiding place gets tightly packed, hence the name of the game.

The last child to find the hiding place becomes the sardine for the next game.

What's in the bag?

Age range 3+
Number of players 4–6
Ideal for Small family gatherings or parties
What you will need Ten plastic bags and items to fill them, pencil and paper for each player

This is an easy game to play, but adults might need to help any very young children unable to write. Children enjoy trying to guess what is in the bags in the same way that they like feeling everybody's presents at Christmas time.

Preparation
Find ten familiar objects the children should be able to recognize by feeling them through a plastic bag, and put one into each bag. Tie the bag so that it is impossible to see inside, and attach a label to each bag numbered 1 to 10. Prepare a sheet of paper for each child with the numbers 1 to 10 written down the left-hand side.

How to play
Each child is given one of the bags, with a sheet of paper and pencil with which he writes his name on the sheet. He is asked to guess by feeling the bag what is inside. He then writes his guess against the appropriate number on the sheet (or he whispers to an adult who writes it down for him). When all the children have made their guesses, they are handed the next bag until each child has guessed the contents of each bag.

When all the guesses are made, the bags are opened one by one and the contents shown. The child who guessed the identity of most objects is the winner.

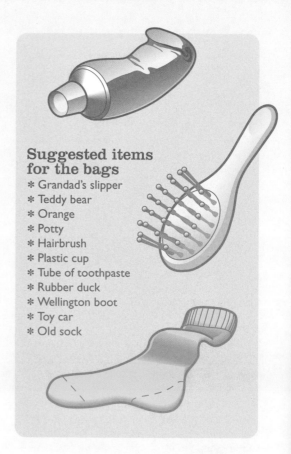

Suggested items for the bags
* Grandad's slipper
* Teddy bear
* Orange
* Potty
* Hairbrush
* Plastic cup
* Tube of toothpaste
* Rubber duck
* Wellington boot
* Toy car
* Old sock

WARNING
When opening the plastic bags, make sure they are collected up, as they can be dangerous around young children.

Pin the tail on the donkey

Age range 3+
Number of players Any
Ideal for Small children's gatherings
What you will need A good-sized pinboard, a piece of cardboard, wool (optional), a blindfold

This is a quiet game which nevertheless provides plenty of amusement for young children.

Preparation

Draw a large donkey without its tail on a sheet of paper and pin it to the pinboard. Unless you are a good artist, it's best to copy a drawing of a donkey from a book. Colour in the donkey and mark a black spot at the point where the tail should hang. Make a donkey's tail from cardboard, coloured as the donkey. Otherwise a circular piece of cardboard with lengths of wool stuck on makes a good donkey's tail. The top end of the tail should have a drawing pin piercing the cardboard so that the tail can be pinned to the drawing.

How to play

The pinboard with the donkey is propped upright, and in turn the children stand a few paces away from the donkey, are handed the tail and then blindfolded. They then have to step forward and pin the tail on the donkey, trying to place it in its correct position. Their efforts will usually cause laughter among the others.

When the tail is pinned, the blindfold is removed and the child surveys his handiwork. An adult then removes the tail and draws a circle round the pinhole, writing against it the name of the child.

When all children have had a turn, the child whose pinhole is nearest to the black spot is · declared the winner.

Buried treasure

Age range 3+
Number of players Any
Ideal for A large party of children, especially of mixed ages

This is a perfect game to keep a large group of children amused. They will love the thrill of looking for buried treasure, especially the eventual winner who gets to keep the 'treasure'.

Preparation

Draw and colour a map like the one illustrated, divided into squares as shown, with the lines of the grid marked 1 to 10 on the left and right and A to J on the top and bottom. (If it is more convenient to have a rectangular map, then do so. The main requirement is that there are about twice as many small squares into which children might stick flags as there are children). Pin the map to the pinboard, and give it the heading Treasure Island.

Cut out as many small pieces of paper as there are children to attend the party and write on

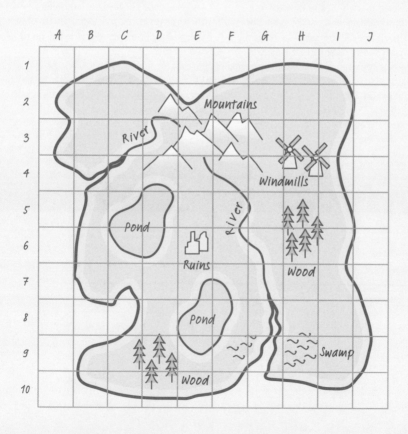

What you will need A pinboard, a large sheet of card or strong paper (such as the reverse side of a sheet of wallpaper), paints or coloured pencils, several drawing pins (one for each child), a prize (the treasure)

each piece the name of a child. You might need to add to this on the day of the party if unexpected children arrive. Stick a drawing pin through each slip so that the head of the drawing pin is on the same side as the name. Drawing pins with coloured heads make the whole thing more attractive.

You have to decide in advance the square on the map in which the treasure is buried. To make the treasure hunt more exciting, you should write the winning square on a piece of paper and place it in an envelope, which should be marked 'treasure hunt winning square'. Pin it to a corner of the pinboard. The description should identify the winning square by letter and number, for example D4 or H7.

How to play

Give each child the drawing pin to which its name is attached and ask them to pin it onto one of the squares on the map of the treasure island where they think the treasure is hidden. Tell them that at a certain time the envelope will be opened to reveal where the treasure is buried. This could be after tea, say, when the opening of the envelope and presentation of the treasure will provide a diversion while others are clearing up the tea-time debris.

Once the winning square is revealed, point it out on the map and indicate the pin that is nearest. The child whose name is attached wins the treasure.

Suitable treats

The 'treasure' should be suitable to the party, of course – worth winning but not worth causing disappointment to those who miss it. It should be suitable for both boys and girls and the age range – say a tin of sweets or box of chocolates.

To make the announcement of the winning square more imposing, you could incorporate it into a rhyme. For example:

*'In the row numbered 4
And the column marked D
That, my friends,
Is where the treasure be.'*

Feeding the baby

Age range 3–5
Number of players Any even number (in teams of two)
Ideal for Parties of very young children
What you will need One spoon for each player and half that number of bowls, small sweets

This game provides fun and amusement for young people and they also get the pleasure of eating something nice (unless you wanted to be cruel and fill the bowls with things that are good for them, like vegetables).

Preparation
Fill your bowls with something nice to eat such as sweets, broken up pieces of chocolate or crumbled cake.

How to play
This game is best supervised by an adult or two to ensure the rules are followed.

Split the party into teams of two (boy–girl is perhaps best where possible) and seat each team beside a bowl of the goodies. Each member of every team is given a spoon.

Tell them that when you say 'Go', each child must feed his or her partner as if they were a baby by spooning food into their mouths. As long as they don't spill any food, the pair that empties its bowl first is the winner.

Age range 3–6
Number of players 6+
Ideal for Getting young players to unite together in a game
What you will need A blindfold

Greetings, O Princess

This is a game children like to play, which has the added benefit of enabling all party members to mix and get to know each other.

How to play
One player is blindfolded (you could use a tie or a clean tea towel).

The other children stand around the blindfolded player. An adult points to one of them who has to walk up to the blindfolded player, take her hand and say in a funny voice 'Greetings O Princess' (if it is a blindfolded boy, of course, the child says 'Greetings O Prince').

Playing with young children
Young children will probably think it more fun to be a princess or prince if they could wear a crown for the part. A strip of cardboard of the thinness used for cereal boxes of about 50 cm (20 in) long and 8 cm (3 in) high is required (you can sticky-tape two pieces together). Cut points into one long side, then stick each end of the strip together to make a crown. Painting it yellow with red rubies would make it look attractive enough for the children to wear with the blindfold.

The blindfolded player has to guess who is holding her hand and speaking. If she guesses right, the two players change places. If she guesses wrong, another child is chosen to approach and say 'Greetings O Princess' and take her hand.

If the blindfolded player guesses wrong three times, she is then replaced by another blindfolded player. The adult should ensure that as many participants as possible have a turn both as the blindfolded player and as the speaker.

Sweet sucking relay

Age range 3–6
Number of players 9+ (in teams of three)
Ideal for Allowing young children to play a game with chocolate sweets (and eat them afterwards)
What you will need Four saucers and three straws for each team, a supply of small chocolate sweets

In this relay game children have to acquire the knack of picking up sweets by sucking them onto the end of a straw, and then to keep them on the end of the straw long enough to pass them to their team-mate.

How to play

Divide the players into teams of three and sit the members of each team side by side, either at a table or on the floor. Each player has an empty saucer in front of him, and there is an extra saucer a little to the left of the third player.

Place in the saucers of the first players of each team a number of sweets (say six or eight). Each team must have the same number of sweets.

On the word 'Go', the first player sucks up a sweet on the end of his straw and drops it into the saucer of the player to his left. As soon as he has done this, he sucks up another and continues until he has passed all the sweets to his partner.

As soon as the second player has a sweet in her saucer she can transfer it in the same way to the saucer of the player to her left. He transfers it to the empty saucer to his left. If a sweet is dropped, it must be picked up and placed back in the bowl from which it came.

The first team to transfer all the sweets from the first saucer to the fourth is the winner.

Age range 3–6
Number of players Any
Ideal for Making young children laugh
What you will need The outer case of a matchbox (a box without its tray) for each player

Matchbox game

This game is more difficult than it looks and will cause some hilarity, first while children try and fail, and again when they succeed and have a matchbox on the end of their noses.

How to play
Get each child to kneel on the floor and then to put their elbows on the floor touching their knees and with their forearms and fingers stretched out before them. About 2.5 cm (1 in) from the end of their fingers stand up a matchbox.

On the word 'Go', the players must put their hands behind their backs and without moving their knees they must lean forward and pick up the matchbox on the end of their noses.

The first to do it wins, but the supervising adult should encourage all who succeed to stay on their knees wearing their matchboxes until all the other players are wearing their matchboxes. If any child can't do it, then stick his matchbox on his nose for him!

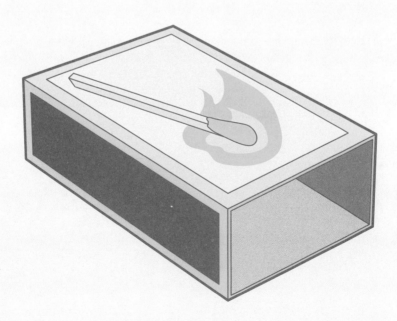

Musical chairs

Age range 5+
Number of players 6–12
Ideal for Entertaining a group of active children

This is a boisterous game that children love, but you must be prepared for an occasional argument, somebody falling over and possibly even a tantrum. Just keep your fingers crossed that there's no damage to the chairs.

Preparation

You need one fewer chairs than there are children taking part. There are two main ways to arrange the chairs. One is in a circle, with the backs of the chairs facing inwards and spaces between the chairs, say roughly the width of two chair-spaces. The other is to arrange the chairs in a row, with alternate chairs facing in opposite directions. Both arrangements are illustrated.

How to play

The children spread themselves out around the chairs, as shown. An adult switches on some music, which is the signal for the children to begin dancing round the chairs. It is best that the person playing the music is out of sight, because at intervals he must stop the music without warning, and it would spoil the game if the children could see when this takes place.

Variation

If you can rustle up enough of them, hats make a good addition to the game. They need not fit the children's heads; in fact, the funnier they look the better. Each hat is put onto one of the chairs, and before sitting on the chair the child must grab the hat off it and sit down putting the hat on. If one child grabs the hat while another sits on the chair, you must give preference to the child with the hat, since the hat must have been taken before the chair was sat upon.

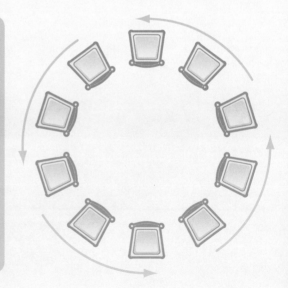

The chairs can be arranged in a circle.

What you will need A number of chairs, a means of playing music (a record, tape or CD player)

When the music stops, each child sits down on the nearest chair. As there is one more child than there are chairs, one child will be left standing. This is where there must be adult supervision since there will often be arguments with two children sitting on the same chair, and an umpire's decisions will be necessary.

The child left standing is eliminated from the game, one chair is removed and the music is restarted. The game continues until eventually only one child is left, and he or she is the winner.

Musical bumps

This is a variation that does not require chairs. The children skip in little jumps to the music and when it stops they must immediately flop to the floor and sit cross-legged. The last to do so is out. This, of course, requires impartial and keen-eyed refereeing, and you will be lucky if there isn't a sulk or two.

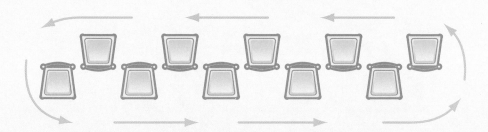

As a variation, you could also arrange the chairs in two lines.

Musical statues

Age range 5+
Number of players Any
Ideal for Parties with a number of over-energetic children

This is a game where you can take your time eliminating the children, as you do not need to eliminate somebody on every round. It is a game that can follow Musical chairs (see pages 18–19), and you might be able to engineer a different winner and allow some of the younger children to stay in the game longer than perhaps they should.

How to play

As with Musical chairs, an adult, preferably not in the line of vision of the children, plays music to which the children dance. You should encourage them to dance flamboyantly, throwing their arms about. Praise the energetic dancers.

When the music stops, each child must stand still like a statue in whatever pose they are in. You will get some odd poses, with some statues having their arms in the air and others perhaps standing awkwardly on one foot. They are not allowed to

What you will need A means of playing music (a record, tape or CD player)

move until the music starts again. The first one caught moving is out.

You should be the judge of who moves first. However, do not hold up the music for more than a few seconds, and if there isn't any obvious early movement, say 'Very good, I did not spot anyone moving'. At this, the person playing the music should begin it again, and the children continue their dance. Eventually only one child will remain and that child is the winner.

Variation

In this variation, best played if the children are at least 7 or 8 years old, you, as the judge, actually try to make one or more of the children move or giggle. Once the music stops and they are frozen in their poses, you move amongst them trying to provoke a reaction. You do this by initiating their stance, staring at them, pulling a funny face, or saying 'Did I see you move?' The children, of course, being statues, must ignore you completely. If one does move or laugh you say 'Sorry, you're out, go and stand over there and help me be a judge in the next round'. You should not be too harsh in your judging at this stage and not spend too long at it, since a child caught in an awkward pose, like standing on one leg, cannot be expected to maintain it for long. As soon as all the children have resisted your efforts for a few seconds, ask for the music to start again.

Keeping them all interested

One way to keep the children involved once they've been knocked out is to invite them to join you as judges. If little Isobel is knocked out first, you can prevent her throwing a fit by saying 'Never mind, Isobel, you can come and stand with me and help me be a judge because I cannot keep my eyes on everybody at once'. When you eliminate the next person, make Isobel feel she is part of it by saying 'I think Sammy moved then don't you, Isobel? Sorry Sammy, you're out, but you can come over here and join Isobel and me as judges'.

When you have a few fellow judges, ask them if they saw anybody move. You do not necessarily have to follow the advice. You can always say 'No, I was watching him. I don't think he moved. Let's carry on with the music'. With luck, all the children will participate until the end.

Pass the parcel

Age range 5+
Number of players Any
Ideal for Entertaining young children, with the prospect of a prize
What you will need A means of playing music (a record, tape or CD player), three or four sheets of wrapping paper, a small prize

This is a traditional game which many of the children will know already.

Preparation

Take the prize, which may be a small box of sweets or the like, and wrap it in a piece of the wrapping paper, using just enough paper to wrap it adequately. Seal the package with something easily removed, such as one piece of sticky tape, or if the shape of the package allows, two elastic bands. The idea is that one layer of packaging can be removed by the children without tearing any layers below.

Continue to re-wrap the package, alternating the patterns of wrapping paper and sealing each layer until the prize has been wrapped up at least a dozen times.

How to play

The children sit around in a circle and one is given the package. When the music starts, the parcel is passed, usually to the right, from child to child. When the music stops, the child holding the parcel unwraps the first layer of wrapping. The music resumes, the parcel is passed again and each time the music stops, the child holding the package unwraps one layer.

Eventually the last layer is unwrapped to reveal the prize, which the child who unwrapped it keeps.

Give all a chance

In this game, it helps if the adult operating the music can see the children so can continue to give as many of them as possible a chance to unwrap a layer. Another supervising adult will need to see that nobody holds the parcel too long, and also to decide who unwraps it when the music stops in mid-hand-over.

A variation is sometimes adopted where each layer contains a small prize, say a small packet of sweets, while the final unwrapping reveals a bigger prize.

Age range 5+
Number of players 7+
Ideal for A mixed age group
What you will need A banana and a means of playing music (a record, tape or CD player)

Banana relay

This game requires bluffing and children will enjoy fooling the 'piggy in the middle', but the game can be played by all ages, including adults.

How to play
Somebody is selected by any means (drawing straws, volunteering or being told) to be the first piggy in the middle, while the others sit round him shoulder to shoulder in a circle or semi-circle, with their hands behind their backs. The more in the circle the better: six is about the minimum. One of the players is handed the banana in front of the others.

The person operating the music begins. When the music starts, the player with the banana passes it behind his back to the next player. She in turn passes it on. However, at any stage the player passing the banana on needn't do so. He can fake to pass it on. Of course, the next player must pretend to pass it on, even if he didn't receive it.

The player in the middle cannot see behind the backs of the others, and must try to guess by their movements who actually has the banana.

Any player who has had the banana passed to him (whether he has it or not) can pass it (or pretend to) one way and then pass it (or pretend to) the other way. The player in the middle must decide whether the movement is genuine or fake.

When the music ends, the player in the middle must decide who has the banana. If he is right, he changes places with the player with the banana. If he is wrong, the player with the banana shows it and the music starts again.

If the player in the middle gets it wrong three times, he still changes with the player holding the banana.

Darting fish

Age range 5+
Number of players Any even number
above six (in teams)
Ideal for Introducing a lively element into a
children's party

**This game is not to be taken too
seriously, and it is quite likely that an
adult supervisor will need to intervene
as foul play is almost unavoidable.**

Preparation

You will need to cut out a number of fishes from
sheets of newspaper, one fish for each child. A
recommended size of fish is about 25 cm (10 in)
by 12.5 cm (5 in). Dabs of paint to represent an
eye and a mouth will make the fish look more
lifelike, and if you know in advance the names
of the children attending the party you could
also paint a name on each fish. To be really
professional you could do the painting on both

sides, as it is likely the fish will turn over during
the race.

How to play

Line up the children's fish at one end of the room
and ask each child to kneel behind his or her fish.
Stretch the string across the other end of the
room to represent a finish line.

Hand the children a magazine each. Explain that
they have to use the magazine like a fan to waft
the fish along the floor. With young children it
might be a good idea to give a demonstration.

On the command 'Go', the children attempt to
blow their fish along the floor to the finish line,
the first to get there being the winner.

What you will need Papers and
magazines, string

The children must be told that they are not
allowed to touch the fish, nor can they prod them
with the magazines. Nor must they get in the way
of anybody else's fish. This is where you will have
to exercise some control because the fish will not
always travel in a straight line, and will even fly up
into the air if some particularly rough child starts
to bang his magazine hard on the floor. There will
inevitably be some arguments to sort out which,
unless it gets vicious, will contribute to the fun.

Variations

If you wish, you could make the race
between two teams, so you would need only
two fish. All members of each team will have
their own magazine to fan the fish along. Set
the two fish as far apart as possible, and
warn that if anybody tries to sabotage the
other team by blowing their fish off course
(or even backwards!) that team will be
disqualified.

WARNING

As well as providing a clear floor space
for the racetrack, ensure that there
aren't any ornaments or lamps on
cabinets which might get banged into in the
course of the race.

Sheepdog trials

Age range 6+
Number of players Any even number above six (in teams)
Ideal for Mixed parties of varying ages

This is a game that is played by teams of two, and has the attraction that a child can be paired with an adult.

How to play

First the 'course' has to be arranged. As big a room or clear space as possible should be used. Lay two chairs on their sides against one wall, so that the backs touch the wall and the legs provide an opening into which a person could crawl (see illustration). The chairs make a sheep pen and the person is the sheepdog.

Around the floor, with a reasonable amount of space between them, should be placed a number of objects, perhaps about six. For example, a small cushion, an upturned wastepaper basket, a pile of three or four books, a cardboard box, a wine bottle and a biscuit tin – anything that can be bumped into without causing injury or damage. It is a nice touch, but not essential, if the objects can be labelled 1 to 6, with 6 being nearest the sheep pen and 1 closest to the opposite side of the room.

Teams of two are selected, and one person is the shepherd and the other the sheepdog. The sheepdog is blindfolded, and the object is for the shepherd to guide the sheepdog around the various obstacles in turn and into the sheep pen. The actual course is agreed beforehand (see illustration).

A timekeeper is appointed, and he must keep the time. The sheepdog is positioned at the end of the room nearest obstacle 1, and is allowed to survey the course. He is then blindfolded, turned round three times and asked to kneel on the floor. When the timekeeper is ready (so when the second hand of his watch is at 12 o'clock), he calls out 'Go', and the sheepdog, guided by the shepherd, must find his way to the pen as quickly as possible.

The shepherd is limited in his instructions. He can say only: 'Forward', 'Back', 'Turn left', 'Turn right', 'Stop' and 'Go'. When the sheepdog turns left or right, he is allowed to add phrases like 'A bit more' or 'Not so much'.

If a sheepdog touches an obstacle, ten seconds is added to his total time, but he is only penalized once for each obstacle – if he knocks an obstacle over he is not penalized if he touches it again.

The sheepdog is not penalized for touching the pen on his way in, and he is deemed to have arrived in the pen when he touches the wall between the chair backs.

The time taken by each sheepdog should be written down. The fastest pair is the winner.

The sheepdogs and shepherds can then change places for another round, or the pairings can be changed.

What you will need A large space, various articles to serve as obstacles (such as cushions, books, stools, cardboard boxes, wastepaper baskets, empty wine bottles, a cylindrical biscuit container), some pieces of cardboard for labels, a stopwatch or a reliable watch with a second hand, a blindfold

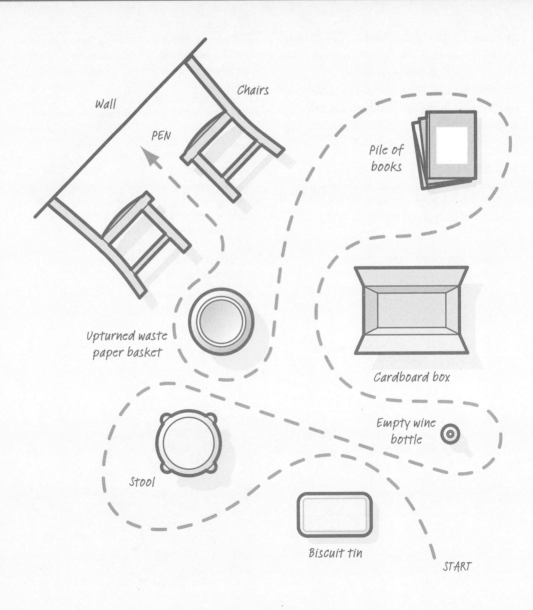

Wall

Chairs

PEN

Pile of books

Upturned waste paper basket

Cardboard box

Stool

Empty wine bottle

Biscuit tin

START

In and out the egg cups

Age range 9+
Number of players 4–12 (in teams)
Ideal for Amusing a group of older children who like a test of skill
What you will need Up to eight egg cups, four table-tennis balls and 12 straws, according to the number of players (see below)

Blowing a table-tennis ball from one egg cup to another is a lot more difficult than it looks, and there will be frustration as well as bouncing table-tennis balls in the air before this game is done.

Preparation
This is a team game, and the number of teams and the size of a team will depend upon the number of players. Suggested are:

  * Four players – two teams of two
  * Six players – two teams of three
  * Eight players – two teams of four
  * Nine players – three teams of three
  * Ten players – two teams of five
  * 12 players – four teams of three

You will need two egg cups per team (large enough to hold a table-tennis ball comfortably), one table-tennis ball per team and one straw per player.

How to play
The teams sit on opposite sides of a table, one player from each team sitting, and the others standing behind their team-mate. The sitting player places his table-tennis ball in an egg cup in front of him and positions the other egg cup a few centimetres beyond it (the player can choose the distance, and can alter it during the game if he wishes).

On the command 'Go', the first player attempts to blow the table-tennis ball from one egg cup into the other. If the table-tennis ball goes astray, his team-mates can retrieve it and place it back in the egg cup for a further attempt.

Once the table-tennis ball has been successfully blown from one egg cup to the other, then the seated player is replaced by another of his team, who has to perform the feat.

The winning team is the first one in which all its members have succeeded.

Age range 8+
Number of players 8+ (in teams)
Ideal for Birthday parties with lots of children of the same age – as many as 16 players can easily be accommodated
What you will need As many chairs as there are children, a small paper bag for each child

Bang bang relay

This game requires a lot of room and might equally well be played outdoors as well as indoors. Children love to make a noise and banging paper bags is always enjoyable, particularly these days when plastic packaging provides fewer opportunities to do so.

How to play
The players are divided into two equal teams. Two rows of chairs are arranged facing each other with about 1.8–2.4 m (6–8 ft) between them. There also needs to be a bit of space at the back of the chairs. On each chair is a paper bag.

Each player sits on a chair (and on the bag). On the command 'Go', the player in chair 1 (see illustration) takes off in the direction shown, runs round the back of his own team's chairs and back to his place. He then picks up his paper bag, sits on his chair, blows up the bag and bangs it.

Extra baggage
It might be an idea to have at least double the number of bags as players. First, you might need to bang one to show youngsters how it's done, and second, the pleasure of banging paper bags is such that the children might want to repeat the game. Poppers or streamers could be used as an alternative to paper bags.

The bang is the signal for the second player to take off, and he runs round the chairs in the same direction, sits, blows up his bag and bangs it, at which point the third player takes off and so on. The team whose last player bangs his bag first is the winner.

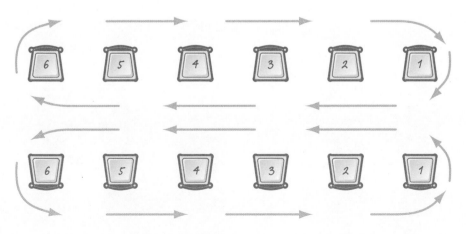

Pass the orange

Age range 5+
Number of players 8+ (in teams)
Ideal for Parties of all ages
What you will need Two oranges

This is a well-known game which promotes a certain closeness between the players. It can be very annoying when the course is almost completed and the orange is dropped, meaning the whole team has to start again.

How to play
Two teams are selected. Some suggest that taller players should form one team and shorter players the other, but it is not necessary – if tall players have to bend, that can add to the fun. The teams need not be equal, but if one team has an extra player it should be the 'stronger' team, as an extra player is a disadvantage.

The teams form up in two lines. The first player in each team is given an orange, which she places under her chin, holding it between chin and neck.

On the command 'Go', the first player transfers the orange from beneath her chin to beneath the chin of the next player. It must not be handled. The second then transfers it to the third, and so on.

If the orange is handled or drops to the floor, it must be passed back to the first player and the whole process started again. When the last player has the orange safely under her chin, she runs or walks back to the first player and transfers it.

When the first player has the orange back, she raises her hand. The first team leader to raise her hand is the winner.

Variation
This similar game can be played for 12, 16 or 20 players as a relay.

Two teams are chosen and this time each team must be of an even number because the teams must be split into pairs. Each pair should be of more or less equal height.

One pair from each team begins at one end of the room with an orange wedged between their foreheads. On the command 'Go', they must run (or walk or waddle) to the opposite wall, touch it and waddle back. If the orange is dropped, they must return to the start line and begin again.

When one pair has successfully negotiated the course, the next pair places the orange between their foreheads (they can do this by hand) and does the same. The winning team is the first to have all its pairs complete the course.

Age range 7+
Number of players 8+ (in teams)
Ideal for Parties of all ages
What you will need A drinking straw for
each player and a packet of tissues.

Straw and tissue race

**In this game the players come close to
each other and have to synchronize their
breathing. It can be infuriating when
the tissue is dropped and floats gently
to the floor.**

How to play

There are two teams of equal numbers, and each
team arranges itself into a line, or a circle. Each
player is provided with a straw, and the leader of
each team is given a tissue. The tissue is unfolded,
and the leader puts one end of his straw into his
mouth, places the tissue over the other end, and
draws in his breath so that the tissue is sticking
to the end of his straw.

On the command 'Go', the leader has to transfer
the tissue to the second player in the team, who
is ready with her straw in her mouth to take it.
She puts the other end of her straw to the tissue
and inhales so that the tissue becomes attached
to her straw. At the same time the leader must
cease inhaling and gently exhale so that the tissue
becomes free of his straw. There is a delicate skill
in the timing.

When the tissue is safely passed, the second
player turns to the third and passes the tissue on
in the same way. The first team to transfer the
tissue to the last player is the winner.

At no time must the tissue paper be touched by
hand, unless it falls to the floor while being
transferred. In this case the player who had it last
must pick it up, reattach it to his straw, and pass it
to the following player as usual.

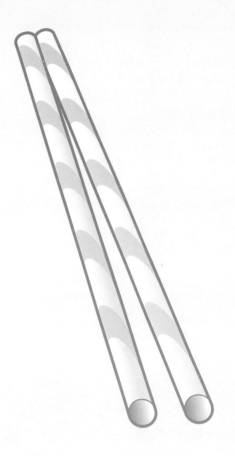

Coming or going?

Age range 6+
Number of players 10+ (in teams)
Ideal for Parties where all ages are
represented, such as at Christmas

**This game can be played in a boisterous
fashion or as a more sedate game. It can
be played either standing up or sitting
down.**

How to play

Two teams are chosen. In this game the more
players the better, so 14 or more is best, making
two teams of at least seven players.

The two teams stand in rows, facing each other,
with about 1.8 m (6 ft) between them. The two
team leaders stand opposite each other. Just in
front of each leader is a bowl full of various
objects, and just behind him is an empty bowl.

Sedate variation

Instead of a number of different objects, you
could instead use a number of pebbles or
coins. In this case each team starts with, say,
20 pebbles, and the team leader counts them
back in to know when the game is over.

If you seek a funny game (and why not – it's a
party) you can express your humour in the
objects, which are going to be passed up and
down the team. You can make them amusing in
themselves – a bra, an old sock, a lavatory chain,
a wig – or you can make them awkward or
surprising to hand – a bar of wet soap, a peeled
banana, a hot potato or a bag of ice cubes.
Some of the items you can duplicate, so that
there is one in each team's bowl. Other things
might be in one team's bowl only. Each team
must have the same number of items, and it's
best if there are at least twice as many items
as team members.

On the command 'Go', each team leader picks
up one object from his bowl and passes it to
the team-mate next to him. As soon as he has

What you will need Four large receptacles such as washing-up bowls or casserole dishes, plus a number of assorted objects

Sitting down variation

Instead of the two teams standing, they can sit on chairs. Here the team sits in a line behind each other, as if on a bus. The team leader passes objects back with his right hand and the last player passes the object from the right to the left hand behind his chair back; he returns it with his left hand down the other side of the line of chairs.

passed it on, he picks up another and passes it on. When an object gets to the end of the line, the last person must pass it round his body and start returning it behind his back. So at one stage of the game there will be objects being passed one way in front of the players and the other way behind them, so some dexterity is required.

If an object is dropped, it must be retrieved and passed on its way. There is no added time penalty.

When the objects start arriving back to the team leader, he takes them behind his back and puts them into the empty bowl. He must remember the last item he passed up so that when it returns to him he can raise his arm to show the team has finished. The first to do so is the winner. If a repeat is required, the teams can swap bowls.

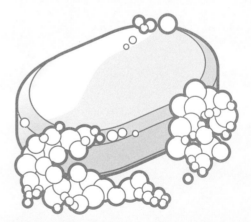

Emptying the sock

Age range 5+
Number of players 6+ (in teams)
Ideal for Youngish children
What you will need Two large opaque men's socks (hiking socks would be ideal), a number of small objects (two of each), ten large pieces of card

In this game children rummage about in a sock to find items by touch. You will need to have plenty of items in the sock otherwise they will find them too easily.

Preparation

Number the cards to make scorecards. The object is to make cards that can register the team's scores from 0–0, to 9–8. One card carries the number 0 on one side and 1 on the other, the next 1 and 2, the next 2 and 3 and so on, the last being 9 and 0. From these you can make any two scores provided both teams don't pass 8.

Fill the two socks with identical small objects. You'll need about three more objects than there are in a team. These objects could be things like a button, a pebble, a large coin, a comb, a sweet, a pencil, an eraser, a toothbrush, a plastic cup or a child's dummy. Keep a checklist of what's in the socks.

How to play

Choose two teams and seat them in two lines. Hand the first child in each line a sock. Call out an object from your checklist. The players have to rummage in the sock (but they can't look in it) and must find the object by feel. They can take out only one object at a time. The first to hold up the correct object scores a point for the team.

Once a player has correctly found an object, take it from her, and also take the equivalent object from the other team's sock, so that the contents of the two socks are again the same.

The two socks are then passed to the second player in each team and you announce another object. Each time an object is found, mark the score for all to see with your two scorecards. When each member of the team has had a turn (or two turns if there are enough objects), you announce the score and name the winning team.

Note that it is important to have a few more items than team members, otherwise the last two or three participants to rummage would find the task too easy.

Age range 6+
Number of players 6+ (in teams)
Ideal for A large number of children, with the more the better
What you will need Two large fruits such as melons or grapefruits

Tutti frutti footy

This is a racing game where fruit is passed by the legs. It is not easy to pass a heavy fruit like a melon to each other without using the hands. You could cut up the fruit afterwards and share it among the players.

How to play

Two equal teams face each other sitting on the floor with their legs stretched out before them. They should sit shoulder-to-shoulder and there should be about 90 cm (3 ft) between one team and the other.

The first player in each line has a fruit, say a grapefruit, placed on her ankles. On the command 'Go', she has to lift her feet and transfer the grapefruit to the ankles of the next player, who passes it similarly to the third, and so on. If the grapefruit rolls off and touches the floor, it has to be returned to the first player and the whole thing started again.

The team to get its grapefruit onto the ankles of the last in the line is the winner.

When both teams have completed the course, have a second race with the grapefruit being passed back in the opposite direction.

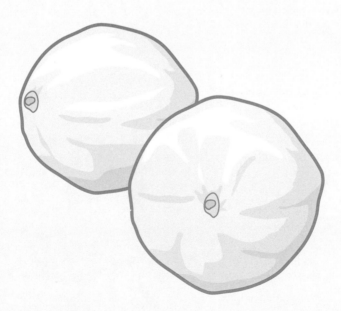

Ex-straw-dinary

Age range 7+
Number of players 6+ (in teams)
Ideal for A quiet interlude at a children's party
What you will need A straw for each child, two thimbles

This is a game requiring that increasingly uncommon item, a thimble; in fact, two thimbles. However, variations are possible if your house is free of thimbles.

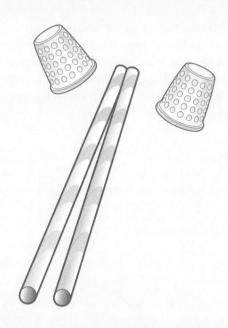

How to play

Two equal teams are seated in rows facing each other, about 1.8 m (6 ft) apart. Each player has a straw. The first player of each team puts the straw in his mouth, pointing it upwards; a thimble is then placed upon it. On the command 'Go', he passes the thimble onto the straw in the next player's mouth. If the thimble is dropped, he must pick it up again using only the straw.

The thimble is passed in this fashion from team-mate to team-mate, and the first team to get its thimble on the straw of the last player is the winner.

WARNING

As this game involves players putting straws in their mouths, it really is not suitable for young children.

Variations

The game can also be played with sweets that have a hole in the middle, passing them on cocktail sticks or toothpicks. Naturally, the proximity of lips can become very close, so this is not encouraged for teenagers.

A second variation is for the players to hold dessert spoons in their mouths and pass on table-tennis balls. In both cases, a dropped sweet or table-tennis ball may be picked up by hand.

Age range 8+
Number of players 8+ (in teams)
Ideal for Children of an age to be able to make a string of paper clips by feel
What you will need A number of standard paper clips (which exceeds the number of players)

Paper clip chain

This is a game that might be frustrating for some young children, so watch out for a sulk and be prepared to accept a little cheating.

How to play

Two equal teams sit in lines on two rows of chairs facing each other. The first in line at one end is handed two paper clips, the other members of the team one each. All must hold their paper clips behind their backs.

On the command 'Go', the first player in the team, with his hands behind his back, joins his two paper clips together. He then hands them, behind his back, to the next player, who adds his paper clip to the chain and passes it on likewise.

When the last player has added his paper clip, the chain is then passed back, in front of the players, to the player who started the chain. At this stage the supervising adult should check that the completed chain has the correct number of links. If any are dropped, they must be found and the leader must attach them behind his back.

The leader then takes the chain behind his back again and unclips one clip, passing the chain on. The last player should receive a chain of two clips, which he unclips and holds the two clips up, whereupon all the others in his team hold up their one clip.

The first team to achieve this wins, but if any clips are missing the other team wins, provided they complete the course satisfactorily.

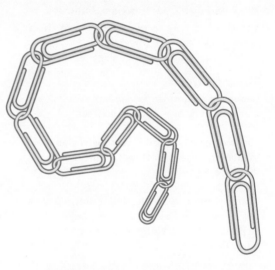

Demonstration

Before the game, it might be advisable for an adult to demonstrate how to clip the paper clips together to form a chain.

Balloon race

Age range 5+
Number of players 8+ (in teams)
Ideal for Young children who like balloons
What you will need Two balloons (plus spares)

Most children's parties have balloons, and this is a way to use a couple of them in a game.

How to play

Two teams are formed and each team lines up in a row, with one player behind another.

The front players in each team are handed a balloon of a different colour (so that they can shout 'Come on red' and 'Come on blue').

On the command 'Go', the first player passes the balloon over her head to the player behind, and he passes it back similarly until it reaches the last player in the line.

The last player runs with the balloon to the front of the line and passes it back through his legs. When it reaches the end of the line, the last player runs to the front and passes it back over his head.

This continues with the balloon being passed back alternately over the head and between the legs until the original leader of the line is back at the front. The first team to achieve this is the winner.

Age range 5+
Number of players 8+ (in teams)
Ideal for Keeping young children entertained and busy
What you will need Two plates, four hard-boiled eggs (plus one or two in reserve in case of breakage); in the absence of eggs, table-tennis balls will do

Your eggs, Sir

This is a fun team game in which the objects you use can be eaten. With luck the children will not tread hard-boiled egg into your carpet, and if the eggs remain intact somebody is bound to eat them during the party. Nothing is wasted!

How to play
The children are formed into two equal teams, each team in a line, one player standing behind the other.

The first child in each line is handed a plate upon which are two hard-boiled eggs. On the command 'Go', she weaves in and out between her team-mates to the back of the line, making sure to go round the last person, and then runs back to the front again. She hands the next player in the team the plate of eggs, saying 'Your eggs, sir' or 'Your eggs, madam'. He then runs to the back of the line while the next player weaves in and out in turn.

The first team to have all its players back in their original positions, with the leader at the front holding the plate of eggs, is the winner.

Putting baby to bed

Age range 12+
Number of players 8+ (in teams)
Ideal for Parties with a number of people approaching teenage; older people can take part too

This game will liven up any family gathering. It can be hilarious. If older people take part (for instance at a Christmas party) care should be taken over the state of their inebriation.

How to play

Two teams are formed and they stand in two lines, one behind the other at one end of the room. At the other end of the room are two chairs, one for each team (one table would suffice if you didn't want to risk your chairs). Neatly arranged on each chair is a glass, a jug of water, a doll and a folded shawl.

On the command 'Go', the first in line of each team rushes to his team's chair, takes the jug and fills the glass to the marked level. He then wraps the doll in the shawl and, taking 'baby' and glass, runs round the back of his team and back to the chair. If during all this the water spills, he must go back to the chair, refill the glass and begin his run again.

When he has completed his run successfully, he empties the glass back into the jug, puts the glass back on the chair, unwraps and replaces the 'baby', folds the shawl and replaces it and runs back to his team. Then he touches the next in line and retires to the back of the line. The next in line then repeats the exercise.

The first team to have all its members complete the run is the winner.

There should be a judge who must see that all the actions are performed properly – that the shawl was folded, for example – between each run.

> **! WARNING**
> There is, of course, a danger attached to this game. Somebody could fall and slip on the water, so there should be at least one sober and responsible adult keeping an eye on affairs.

What you will need Two plastic glasses, two plastic jugs of water, two dolls, two small shawls

Variations
There are several ways to adapt this game. You could try running with an egg and spoon instead of the glass of water, or even going on hands and knees with an oiled groundsheet in front of the chair.

Hide and seek

Age range 6+
Number of players Any
Ideal for Parties of young children
What you will need A house with lots of potential hiding places, and a watchful eye to make sure children don't wander where they shouldn't; the game can also be played outside

Hide and seek is a game that hardly merits description, since all children know it from a young age. However, it is surprising how old some children get before they grasp the idea of hiding themselves. Even when they have 'got it', they often cannot stay hidden long – they need to be in the action.

How to play

One child is the seeker. She stands in a corner facing the wall with her eyes shut and counts to 50 while the others hide about the house. On reaching 50, she calls 'I'm coming' and goes off to seek. Anyone found retires from the game, and the game ends when all are found. The first to be found becomes the seeker for the next game. If before being found a hider can slip back to the starting corner without being seen and call out 'I'm home', the game ends and the seeker has to be the seeker again.

One, two, three, four ... fifty!

I'm coming!

Variation

One person can hide, while all the others become seekers. The seekers remain in the room and count up to 50 while the 'fugitive' hides. The seekers then split up and hunt for the fugitive. The seeker who finds the fugitive becomes the fugitive next time round.

! WARNING
There might be places where you do not want young children to hide, such as wardrobes containing expensive clothes. You should make sure the players know of any 'out of bounds' places before they set off.

Age range 6–10
Number of players Any
Ideal for A party of youngsters where a quiet interlude would be welcomed
What you will need A room containing plenty of objects

I-spy

This is a game in which children need to know how to spell. If any participants are not able to spell, the sound of the first letter can be given rather than the letter itself.

How to play

The children sit in a room together. One of them chooses any object in the room that is visible to all, and cries out 'I spy with my little eye, something beginning with...' And she names a letter.

The other children look round and name things they can see beginning with that letter. The first to guess the chosen object becomes the chooser for the next round.

If the game goes on too long, a supervising adult should suggest that a clue be given, and ask questions intended to narrow the field. These could include 'Is it hanging on the wall?' 'Is it on the floor?' 'Is it on a cabinet?' 'Could you tell us its colour?' or 'Is it make of wood?'

If the object still remains unguessed, there is the possibility that the child has made a mistake and that the object doesn't begin with the letter announced at all, so the supervisor should suggest that everybody gives in.

The chooser then announces the object and is allowed to choose another. If a mistake has been made, it can be tactfully pointed out (and any derision of the other children halted) and the chooser can still have another turn.

... R

... B

... H

... J

... S

Department store

Age range 8+
Number of players 8+ (in teams)
Ideal for A game for all ages which promotes fun and cooperation
What you will need The cooperation of players who might be required to take off their socks or bracelets

This is based on an adult game where players have to supply the customer from their own resources, no matter how intimate the required items might be. Children can collect items from anybody present, as they will not be expected to have them all.

How to play

Two teams are chosen, one positioned at one side of the room, one at the other. The teams should each contain old and young, males and females. They represent department store assistants.

A customer (you or another adult) enters with a shopping list (which for convenience could be prepared in advance). He sits halfway between the teams and reads out the things he wants, one item at a time. The first person to bring the item to the customer scores a point for her side.

Items could be what the teams might have on them (a pair of shoes, a wristwatch) or they could be something that will have to be found and brought from within the house.

Only those under a certain age (you must decide what it is, with your players in mind) can bring things to the customer, so if a watch is demanded, an adult must give it to a child to deliver.

Tick off the shopping list with ticks for one side and crosses for the other. The team with the most points wins. An odd number of items on the shopping list will ensure a winner.

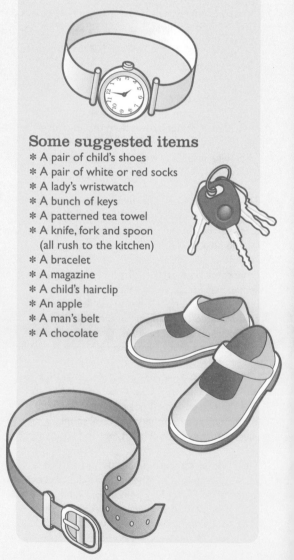

Some suggested items
* A pair of child's shoes
* A pair of white or red socks
* A lady's wristwatch
* A bunch of keys
* A patterned tea towel
* A knife, fork and spoon (all rush to the kitchen)
* A bracelet
* A magazine
* A child's hairclip
* An apple
* A man's belt
* A chocolate

Age range 8-12
Number of players Any
Ideal for A quiet interlude with children, where the only noise made is sniffing
What you will need Ten plastic or paper bags with holes in them, ten strongly smelling objects, pencils and paper

Bloodhounds

This is called a hunting game because the players pretend to be bloodhounds, identifying items by their smell.

Preparation
Find ten quite small but strongly smelling objects such as a sprig of lavender or a piece of Camembert cheese, and put each into a bag with small holes to release the smell. Tie the bags and place them at intervals around the edge of a table, numbering them by means of a piece of paper 1 to 10. Draw up a sheet of paper with the numbers 1 to 10 written down the left-hand side.

How to play
Give each player a prepared sheet of paper and a pencil. The players walk round the table attempting to identify each smell and writing what it is on their sheets. They are not allowed to touch the bags. When everyone has been round the table, open the bags and show everybody the contents. The player with the most correct guesses is the winner.

Some suggested items
* Lavender
* Curry powder
* A strong-smelling cheese
* A bar of soap
* A cut onion
* A piece of rag or cotton wool soaked in vinegar
* A cut orange, or some peel
* A very smelly sock
* Some chocolate sweets
* A few strong peppermint sweets

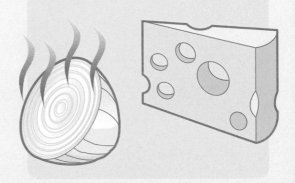

Find the other half

Age range 6+
Number of players Any
Ideal for Getting people at a party to get to know each other
What you will need The pictures from some of your old Christmas cards

This is a game that will help your guests get to know each other as they have to mingle. It will eventually provide two 'winners'.

Preparation

In a way, this needs planning well in advance because you need a stock of old Christmas cards. Take those of a more or less equal shape and size, cut off the front (containing the picture) and cut each picture in half. Each guest at the party will need half a card, so you can estimate how many cards to cut up.

How to play

Each player is given half of a Christmas card. If you have an even number of players, you must ensure that two of those halves will not match up with another half. All the players then mingle and try to find the player with the other half of their card. When they do, they bring both halves to you and go into the next round. When all cards are

Odd number of players

If you start with an odd number of players, you will want to eliminate one only on the first round, so distribute just one half-card that cannot be matched. After the first round, proceed as above, eliminating two players each round.

matched up, there will be left the two players who had the unmatched cards. They are eliminated. You then shuffle the cards, remove one and repeat the exercise for those still playing, remembering to ensure that two halves of cards are unmatched. Change the two unmatched half-cards each round. Two players get eliminated each round, and the last pair are the winners.

Age range 4–6
Number of players 8+
Ideal for Young children to take part in a simple guessing game
What you will need A child's shoe

Hunt the shoe

If you are hosting a party for very young children, you can get them together into a manageable state with this game.

How to play

All but one of the children sit in a circle as close as possible to each other, the odd one sitting in the centre. The child in the centre is given a shoe. All the children (including the one in the centre) recite the following rhyme:

'Cobbler, cobbler, mend my shoe,
Have it done by half past two.'

While this is being recited, the child in the centre hands the shoe to one of the children in the circle. She then closes her eyes and covers them with her hands.

The children now start passing the shoe from one to another behind their backs round the circle. As they are doing this, all recite:

'Cobbler, cobbler, tell me true,
Which of you has got my shoe?'

Whoever is holding the shoe when the word 'shoe' is reached keeps hold of the shoe behind her back. The centre child then opens her eyes and guesses from the expressions and giggles which child has the shoe. She is allowed two guesses. If she gets it right, she stays in the centre. If not, she changes places with whoever is holding the shoe.

Card for card

Age range 8–12
Number of players Any
Ideal for A party of children who can recognize playing cards
What you will need Two packs of playing cards, a score-sheet

In this game each child has a playing card from one pack of cards and they go round the house searching for the identical card from another pack, which you have hidden.

Preparation

One pack of playing cards, or as many cards as you think necessary for the number of children (about four cards per child) should be placed around the house in easily visible positions. It might be best to restrict the cards to one or two rooms that the children would not go in without invitation, otherwise all the cards will be spotted before you begin the game. Keep a list of the cards distributed and put aside from the other pack of playing cards the equivalent cards to those lying around.

How to play

Give each player a playing card from the second pack and, on the command 'Go', send the children off to find the matching card from those that you have spread around. When a player finds a match to his card, he brings both cards to you and you write his name against that card on your checklist. You then give him another card to try and match.

When all cards are found and returned to you, add up each score and announce the winner.

Age range 8–12
Number of players Any
Ideal for Entertaining children in a quiet manner
What you will need About six lengths of wool of different colours, a tape measure

Gathering wool

This game has the benefit of allowing you to get rid of all those odd lengths of different coloured wool that you've kept for several years and that are never going to be used for anything except this simple children's game.

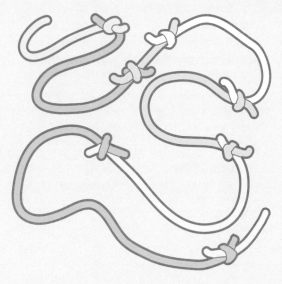

Preparation

The pieces of wool must be cut into lengths, but not necessarily all the same length – anything between 15–30 cm (6–12 in). There should be perhaps six to ten lengths for every child you expect to be playing. These lengths are hidden about the house, where part or all of them can be plainly seen. Locations could include poking out from under a curtain or rug, sticking out from the pages of a book or magazine, hanging from a drawer, curled up on the floor or hanging from a door-knob. Remember they must all be seen (it is unnecessary for anyone to open drawers) and they must be reachable by all.

How to play

Get all the players together (if you have more than eight you might divide them into pairs) and, on the command 'Go', they must go and search for the wool. When they have two pieces, they must immediately be tied together and every

subsequent piece must also be tied on. The object is to get the longest piece of wool, so the knots should be as small as they can be made.

At a given time, call a halt and measure each length of wool to find the winner. If you are giving prizes, there could be a secondary prize for the player who has collected most pieces of the same colour.

Memory game

Age range 7+
Number of players Any
Ideal for Providing a quiet period in parties where players must concentrate

This game tests players' memories. If all your players are of a similar age, you can play the game as individuals. If the players are of differing ages – and it is assumed older people (up to a limit) will be better at it – then the game can be played in teams of two or three, with an older and younger person in each.

Preparation

On a tray, spread out up to 20 small objects and cover them with a cloth.

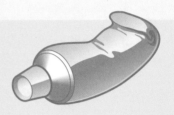

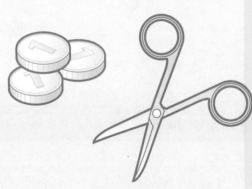

Optional extra

Later in the party, when the items on the tray have been dispersed, you can assemble the teams, hand out pencils and paper, and ask them how many of the original items on the tray they can remember.

Some suggested items

* A watch
* A shoe lace
* A corkscrew
* A pair of nail scissors
* An elastic band
* A screw
* A ball-point pen
* A small photograph
* A key
* A ring
* A coin
* A tube of toothpaste
* A matchstick
* A tin of shoe polish
* A piece of chocolate
* A biscuit
* A walnut
* A marble
* A small piece of string
* A feather

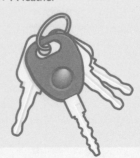

What you will need A large tray, a cloth to cover it, about 20 small objects, paper and pencil for each player (or team), a watch for timing

How to play
Arrange teams if required. Give each individual or team paper and pencil. Produce the covered tray and tell them that you have a tray on which there are a number of objects. Tell them you propose to remove the cloth for 45 seconds, during which time they must remember as many objects as they can. You will then cover the tray again, and they will have four minutes to write down every item they can remember. There is to be no writing down during the memorizing period.

Look at your watch and, at a time suitable to you, uncover the tray. After 45 seconds, cover the tray again, and ask them to write down all the items they can remember. Call time after four minutes and make sure nobody adds to the list after that.

Uncover the tray. The winners are those who have correctly remembered most objects.

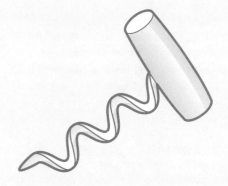

Follow-up game
Collect all the sheets of paper.

Tell your audience you are going to take the tray into the other room for a minute. Do so, and remove about five of the items.

Return with the covered tray. Hand out to each team or individual a fresh sheet of paper. Tell them that you have removed five objects and that when you uncover the tray they have four minutes to write down what they are.

After four minutes, cover the tray and ask if anyone has got all five. If not, ask if anyone has four, then three and so on. The winning team is the one that has correctly remembered most.

What is it?

Age range 9+
Number of players Any (in teams)
Ideal for Entertaining a group of children
over the age of about 9, as well as adults – all
can compete together

This game's success depends mostly on the things you put in the bowls. At best they can inspire bewilderment, squeamishness or horror, but with luck all the players will be fascinated at the denouement.

Preparation

It is best if you can prepare the bowls before the party and keep them out of sight of the players. You should at least have all the items for the bowls ready.

Fill the bowls with things that players can identify by touch. Some can be fairly straightforward: a bowl of paperclips, for example, is easy to identify. Other bowls could have things a bit more difficult, such as unusual breakfast cereal or some blades of grass. Some could contain liquids, pure orange juice, for example, which could be identified by smelling the fingers dipped in it; a bowl might have something slimy in it, like cold custard. If you knew your guests well, you could put a couple of earthworms in a bowl. This should induce some shrieks from some, but of course you'd have to watch that they (the worms) don't escape.

How to play

You will need three or four adults not in the game to help supervise, since the players themselves will be blindfolded.

Set the bowls, each covered with a cloth, around three sides of a table. Tell the players you are going to blindfold them, remove the covers from the bowls, and that they are going to go round the table feeling the contents of each bowl, deciding what is in them, and remembering them. Tell them that as some of the bowls might contain wet or sticky objects you are going to give each a piece of kitchen roll for wiping their fingers. Tell them that also smelling their fingers might help after feeling some things.

Explain that at the end, when all the players have been round, you are going to cover the bowls again and remove their blindfolds. Then they have to write down the contents of as many of the bowls as they can remember.

The player who remembers correctly the contents of most bowls wins. After the game, you can show the contents of the bowls to the players.

What you will need A number of fruit bowls, basins, dessert dishes or the like (preferably a couple or so more than the number of players), various items to fill them (see below) and cloths to cover them with, blindfolds, pencil, paper and a piece of kitchen roll or similar for each player

Some suggested items
* Breadcrumbs
* Holly leaves (prickly)
* Feathers
* Rice pudding (sticky)
* Cut up rubber bands
* Used tea leaves
* Baked beans (slimy)
* Small toy furry mouse
* Nails
* Cherry tomatoes
* Shredded paper
* Sharp sand

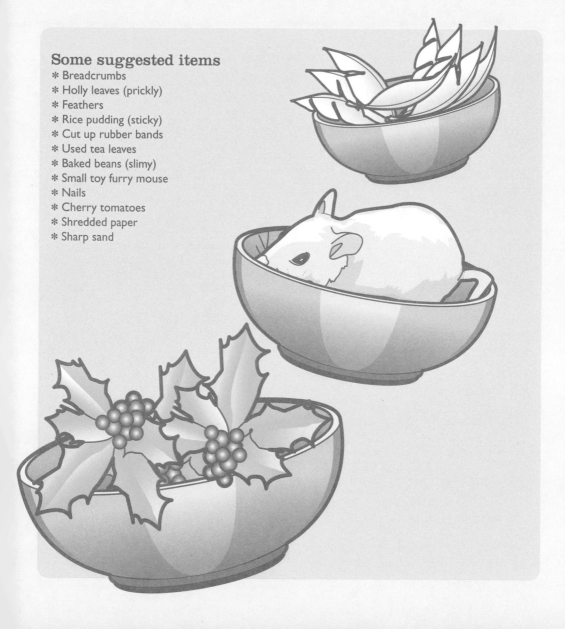

Twenty questions

Age range 9+
Number of players Any (in teams)
Ideal for A party of brainy types

This is a game that ran for many years on the radio and made one or two people quite famous. It is sometimes called 'Animal, vegetable or mineral'.

How to play

Players are divided into two teams (they need not be exactly equal as an extra person on a team doesn't matter). The two teams sit roughly facing each other.

One team is the team setting the puzzle and the other team is the questioning team. The first decides amongst itself on some subject, which can be a person (living or dead, real or fictional), an object or a place. This can be general, for instance 'a shop', or it can be specific, such as the name of an actual shop local to you.

They tell the questioning team whether the subject is animal, vegetable or mineral, or sometimes a combination. Most things come under one of these categories (see panel). It makes it easier if other abstract things are not chosen.

It is also helpful to say how many words there are in the subject to be guessed, and if any are the definite article (the) or indefinite article (a, an). For example if the subject is 'a black cat', you would say 'Animal, three words including the indefinite article'.

Categories

Animal: This covers all animal life, from insects to human beings, and anything that derives from it. Examples: a racehorse, a slug, Britney Spears, milk, a cat's paw, a toe nail, Lassie, a boiled egg, leather shoes.

Vegetable: This covers everything in the realm of plants and trees and things that derive from them. Examples: a chestnut, breakfast cereal, a Christmas tree, mistletoe, carrots.

Mineral: This covers inorganic, inanimate things such as stone, iron, glass and anything made of them. Examples: a Ferrari, the Eiffel Tower, a diamond ring, a horseshoe, the Golden Gate Bridge.

Combination: Sometimes a subject can best be described as a combination, thus Nelson's Column might be said to be 'mineral, with animal connections'.

What you will need An authoritative
manner (or authoritative friend) to cool
down disputes over misleading answers
to questions

The guessing team have 20 questions in which to
find the subject. Each question must be of the
kind that can be answered either 'Yes' or 'No'.

Any of the questioning team can ask a question.
A usual line of questioning, if the subject is animal,
might take the form:

'Is it human?'	*'Yes, one'.*
'Male?'	*'No, two'.*
'Female?'	*'Yes, three'.*
'Living?'	*'No, four'.*
'A particular person?'	*'Yes, five'.*
'Famous?'	*'Yes, six'.*
'In show business?'	*'Yes, seven'.*

And so on. In seven questions, the team will know
they are looking for a dead woman or girl who
was famous in show business.

If the questioning team fails to discover the
subject within its 20 questions, the posing team
thinks of another subject. If the questioning team
succeeds, however, the roles are reversed.

Spoof

Age range 10+
Number of players 3–8
Ideal for A relaxing interval between more exacting games, for instance while taking a drink
What you will need Three identical small objects for each player such as coins, counters, draughtsmen or pebbles

This is a game in which each player guesses how many objects are concealed in the fists of all the players, himself included. Guesses can be high or low, based on other players' guesses, but remember everybody is free to indulge in a bit of bluff.

How to play
All players are given three coins each.

Each player conceals in his fist as many of his three coins as he wishes: the number could be 0, 1, 2 or 3. The object is to guess the total number of coins hidden in the fists of the players.

Any player can volunteer to be first guesser on the first round, after which the privilege of being first guesser passes to the left. All the players then conceal a number of coins in whichever fist they prefer and hold that fist out over the table. Any coins not being held in the fist are held in the other hand under the table. The first player then states how many coins he thinks are held collectively by all the fists on the table. If there are five players, this could be between 0 (all fists holding no coins) and 15 (all holding three). The second player guesses a different number (it is not allowed for two players to guess the same number) and so on until all have guessed. The fists are then opened, and the correct guesser scores a point. If nobody is correct, no points are scored. The first person to reach an agreed number of points is the winner.

Players will tend to call higher or lower according to the number of coins in their own hand, but it sometimes pays to bluff.

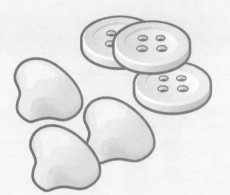

Variation
The game can be played to find a loser rather than a winner. When a player guesses correctly, he drops out. The last player remaining is the loser.

Age range 8+
Number of players 6, 8 or 10 (in two teams)
Ideal for Entertaining a group of boisterous children
What you will need A long table to seat 3, 4 or 5 on each side and a small object like a marble or coin

Up Jenkins!

This is an old-established game requiring a little dexterity and bluffing. It can be quite hilarious.

How to play

Two teams sit on opposite sides of the table. Team captains toss for who is first to bluff. The winning side has the 'tippit' – a small object like a marble.

The tippit is shown to the guessing side and is then passed by the bluffing side from hand to hand under the table, while they try to confuse the other side as to the whereabouts of the tippit. The captain of the guessing side eventually calls 'Up Jenkins!' and all the bluffing side raise their fists into the air. Then the guessing captain calls 'Down Jenkins!' and the fists are dropped to the table, with the back of the hand upwards. The hands are then spread flat, with palms on the table, beneath one of which is, of course, the tippit.

The guessing side now has to guess which hand conceals the tippit. First, half the hands are eliminated by each member of the guessing side pointing in turn to one of the hands he thinks doesn't hide the tippit, and saying 'Take that hand away'. If a hand is chosen that does contain the tippit, then the guessing side has lost. If, however, all goes well, and half the hands are removed, then the captain must choose, after consultation with his team, which remaining hand does hide the tippit.

If the guessing side finds the tippit, it wins and scores a point. It takes over the tippit and becomes the bluffing side. If it fails, the bluffing side scores a point and retains the tippit for the next round. The winning side is the first to an agreed number of points, usually one more than the number of players.

What's in the sock?

Age range 6+
Number of players Any (in teams)
Ideal for Family parties, as all ages can join in
What you will need Two large hiking socks (which cannot be seen through), a number of objects to fill them, two pencils and paper

This is a little like the racing game Emptying the sock (see page 34), but it is not a race – it is designed to test how well players can identify things, and then how good their memory is.

Preparation
Fill the large socks with a number of objects – at least twice as many as there are players. There should be the same number in each sock. Avoid sharp objects.

How to play
Divide the players into two teams (they do not have to be exactly equal). Each team must appoint a captain. Hand a sock to each captain. Each team has five minutes to try to identify and remember as many objects as they can by feel. They can either all feel the sock together and discuss their guesses, or hand the sock round.

After five minutes, tell the teams to keep remembering the objects, and change the socks over. Teams have another five minutes to identify as many objects as they can in the other sock.

After a further five minutes, take the socks and hand out to the captains a pencil and paper. The teams have another five minutes to recall as many objects as possible, while the captain writes them down. It is not necessary to specify which sock the objects were in.

The team with the most correct identifications wins the game.

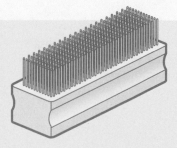

Some suggested items
* A ring
* A pebble
* A watch
* A piece of string
* A toothbrush
* A lipstick case
* A roll of sticky tape
* A coin
* A door key
* A bulldog clip
* A jar of jam
* An orange
* A comb
* A birthday card
* The top of a beer bottle
* A shoe polish tin
* A cork
* A nail brush
* A glasses case
* A plastic cup

Age range 6–8
Number of players Any
Ideal for Sitting children together quietly
for a few minutes
What you will need A long piece of string,
a ring

Ring on a string

This is a quiet, sitting-down game in which the child in the middle must guess which of the other children is holding a ring. The other children try to make it as difficult as possible, of course.

Preparation

A ring is threaded onto a piece of string and the two ends of the string are tied. Make sure the knot isn't too large to allow the ring to pass easily over it.

How to play

The string holding the ring is spread in a circle on the floor. One child is chosen to sit in the middle, while the others sit round her, taking the string

that passes through all their hands. One of the children takes the ring in her fist. The child in the middle knows where the ring is.

On the word 'Go' from a supervising adult, the child holding the ring passes it (or pretends to) to the child next to her, who passes it from one hand to another before passing it on (or pretending to). It can be passed either way, and go backwards or forwards. The child in the centre must try to keep track of the ring, and decide whether any of the passes was faked.

After a few passes, the adult says 'Stop' and the child in the middle must guess who is now holding the ring. If she is correct, she changes place with the ring holder; if wrong, she stays in the middle for another turn. After three unsuccessful turns, another player can volunteer to change places.

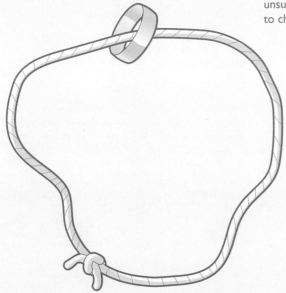

Who am I?

Age range 12+
Number of players Any
Ideal for Mixed-age family parties when the younger children have gone to bed

This is an interesting game which can prove very frustrating. Each player is given an identity which he has to discover by asking questions. It is amazing how difficult it is to guess your own identity when everybody else's seems so easy.

How to play

There is no preparation needed beforehand. Each player is given a sticky note upon which he writes the identity of a well-known character, either real or fictional, alive or dead. The character need not be human – it could be, say, Lassie, or a cartoon character like Bugs Bunny.

Each player places his sticky note on the forehead of another player so that eventually everybody has the name of a character of some sort stuck on their forehead. Each player, of course, knows the identity of every other player, but not their own.

Players arrange themselves roughly in a circle (they usually stay in the armchair they were already sitting in).

One player starts by asking questions of the others with a view to finding out who he is. The questions can only be of the sort to be answered 'Yes' or 'No'. Occasionally, though, the answer is not clear-cut, and the other players must answer as best they can. They must be helpful to the questioner and not deliberately deceive.

While the questioner gets 'Yes' for an answer he continues questioning. If he gets a 'No', his turn passes, and the player on his left begins to ask questions likewise.

Eventually a player feels confident enough to name who he thinks he is, and if he is right he unpeels his sticker and enjoys the admiration of the others. If wrong, his turn passes to the left as usual.

The sort of questions to ask are: 'Am I human?', 'Am I alive?', 'Am I a man?' or 'Am I a celebrity?'

What you will need Sticky notes (one for each player) and a pencil

Some suggested identities
* Harry Potter
* Elizabeth Taylor
* William Shakespeare
* Robin Hood
* Mickey Mouse
* Tony Blair
* Gandhi
* Napoleon
* Woody Allen
* Marge Simpson
* Justin Timberlake
* Charlie Chaplin
* George W. Bush
* Lance Armstrong
* Fred Flintstone
* Pelé

The health of Colonel Bogey

Age range 12+
Number of players Any
Ideal for Entertainment at the end
of a meal

This has its basis in an adult drinking game in which participants might already be somewhat jolly, and is designed to make them even more so. However, it can be enjoyed with some hilarity by persons of all ages, and children will enjoy joining in with their elders at family parties.

How to play

This game needs a toastmaster, or master of ceremonies, or someone who has learnt the routine, which might be you.

It requires everybody sitting round a table with a drink, so is ideal for that period after a meal when everybody is relaxing with a full stomach and a feeling of goodwill – enough goodwill to drink the health of Colonel Bogey. The drink need not be alcoholic, and of course in the case of those below the legal age for alcohol, it must not be.

As toastmaster, you make sure everybody has a full glass of the drink of their choice and tell them that you are going to observe an old ritual in drinking the toast to Colonel Bogey, and that they must all watch and remember what you do because they must join you in doing it afterwards. Explain what you are doing as you go along.

You then say 'Now we are all going to do it', and lead everybody in repeating the above. Do not take your time, or pause for slower participants, or explain further. The enjoyment comes from everybody trying to remember the sequence, and getting it wrong – the more wrong the merrier.

The routine

1 Stand up, pick up your glass with your thumb and index finger (exaggerate the one finger), raise it chin-high, and say 'I drink to the health of Colonel Bogey for the first time'.

2 Take one sip of the drink, sit down and replace your glass on the table with one distinct tap.

3 Wipe your (perhaps imaginary) moustache with the back of your hand, first to the right, then to the left.

4 Tap the table once with your right hand to the right of your glass, then once with your left hand to the left of your glass.

5 Tap the underside of the table once, first with your right hand, then your left.

6 Stamp on the floor, first with your right foot, then with your left.

7 Rise a little from your seat, and then sit down again.

What you will need A plastic glass for all players and the drink of their choice to fill it with

As soon as everybody is seated, stand up again and pick up your glass with your thumb and first two fingers (make sure it is clear you are using two fingers). Lift it to your chin and say 'I drink to the health of Colonel Bogey for the second time'.

You then repeat the procedure as before, but you do everything twice: two distinct sips from the glass, sit down, replace the glass with two taps, wipe each side of the moustache twice, tap the table each side above and below twice, sit up and sit down twice.

Then, with an 'All together now', you make everybody do it. When all are sitting, say 'Stand again, because we're going to do all the rest together'. All together, you drink the health of Colonel Bogey for the third time, performing every action three times.

When that's completed, you say 'Stand. I now drink to the health of Colonel Bogey for the last time'. You all do the last verse, holding the glass with thumb and four fingers, and repeating the actions four times. Go through this verse quickly, and there's a chance that everyone will collapse on their chairs laughing.

> **! WARNING**
> If you think there are one or two of your party who are a little tipsy, you should perhaps point out that this game involves tapping glasses on the table and that anybody who taps too hard will not be allowed another drink all evening.

The killer wink

Age range 8+
Number of players Any
Ideal for Mixed parties of adults and older children, including dinner parties
What you will need A pack of playing cards

This game is best played during a lull, such as if the table has to be cleared or if it's time to pass round a box of chocolates. It can also be played while another game is being prepared or while everybody is talking around the dinner table after a meal.

How to play

The host takes a number of cards from a pack, to equal the number of players. One of the cards must be the Ace of Spades, the card of death.

The cards are shuffled and one is handed face-down to each player. The players secretly look at their cards, without letting anybody else see which card they have, and pass the cards back to the host. One of them will have received the Ace of Spades. He or she is the killer.

As normal activity resumes (such as passing the chocolates or the resumption of chatting), the killer sets about his murders. To commit a murder, the killer must wink at a victim as surreptitiously as possible, hoping nobody else notices. The victim waits a few seconds (so as not to make the identity of the killer obvious) and then, with suitable yells, moans, gurgles, throat clutching or other histrionics, sinks to the floor (or slumps back on his chair) dead. Would-be actors or other exhibitionists will like this part.

The job of the killer is to kill as many as possible without being caught. The killer is caught when another player thinks he has spotted the killer wink at his victim. The spotter announces he knows the killer, at which point all those not dead must close their eyes. The accused then touches the person he thinks is the killer and returns to his place, when everyone can open their eyes. If he is right, the game ends with the killer apprehended, but if he is wrong, he takes no further part in the game and the killer seeks out more victims.

Age range 6+
Number of players Any
Ideal for Getting people to know each other at the beginning of a party
What you will need Sticky notes (one for each player), about eight cocktail sticks or similar small items for each player

Odd or even

This game is a good one for those parties where perhaps some people are meeting others for the first time. It makes everybody circulate and meet each other, addressing each other by name so they soon get to know each other.

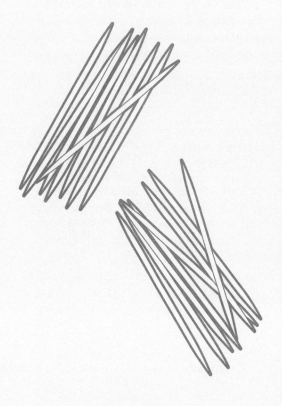

Preparation
Write the name of each party guest on a sticky note (or have a pencil and blank labels handy so guests can write their own names) and arrange your cocktail sticks into piles of eight. In the absence of cocktail sticks, beans or pebbles would suffice.

How to play
Hand each guest the label containing his or her name and a pile of eight cocktail sticks.

Players circulate and, using the label, address each other by their names. Suppose James approaches Sylvia. He takes some or all his sticks in his fist and says to her 'Sylvia, odd or even?' If Sylvia guesses correctly she takes one of James's cocktail sticks. If she is wrong, she hands James one of hers. Then, taking some of her sticks in her fist, she says 'James, odd or even?', and another stick changes hands according to the accuracy of James's guess.

After five minutes or so, when everybody has had time to meet everybody else, the host calls a halt and the player with the most sticks is the winner.

The horror game

Age range 12+
Number of players As many as can comfortably sit round a table
Ideal for A quiet period in a small party

The success of this game relies on the skill of the presenter (you!). So prepare carefully, have a good story ready and play the game only when the atmosphere of the party is right; you want to be sure that you can weave your spell without the likelihood of silly interruptions to break the tension.

> **! WARNING**
> Do not invite young children to take part, and warn others that if they are of a particularly nervous disposition perhaps they should sit this one out.

How to play

Seat the guests around the table. Place a baby wipe in front of each. You, with your box of props, should be at head of the table with your props in a covered box at your feet. Nobody must see the props. The room should be as dark as possible, perhaps with the curtains drawn and lit by a single candle in a corner.

Tell the guests that you have recently discovered some gruesome remains of a body in the loft of your house and that they correspond with a rumour of a murder you heard about some time ago – which you will now relate. You then tell your story in as spine-chilling a manner as you can. A suggested framework follows.

'According to the rumour, a strange man who lived somewhere in this area claimed to have murdered a young tramp, and to escape detection had dismembered the body and hidden some parts of it in a cardboard box which was never found. Well, I found what could be this box in the attic. According to the murderer, he first chopped of the victim's head and then cut out the eyes, and two things in the box look like decaying eyes. I'll pass them round under the table. [You pass round the two tomatoes]. Don't squeeze them too hard, because you don't want eyeball all over your fingers! What do you think? I have to pass them under the table because if you saw the eyes looking at you you'd faint.'

When the tomatoes are nearly back to you, resume the story.

'He also removed the tongue, which I will pass round now. [Pass the piece of rubber round]. As you can feel, it has lost some of its flexibility over the years, and has hardened up a little, but you can still see traces of dried blood round the base. I'll let anyone who wants to examine it do so afterwards, but I warn you, it's not a pretty sight.'

What you will need Some of the following: rubber gloves, a damp sponge, two hard cherry tomatoes, two carrots, two dried figs, a lock of hair, a piece of rubber shaped like a tongue, a beetroot, a towel, a table with an overlapping plastic tablecloth, a candle, a packet of baby wipes

Continue in this manner with the other objects.

The dried figs (or apricots) represent the ears. A lock of hair is, of course, a lock of hair. The squeamish will be especially horrified when you describe how the head was severed so that the killer could keep the brain. You must say, as you pass round the slightly damp sponge:

'Be careful with the brain. Although it has dried out somewhat, it's still a bit squashy and parts might come off and I wouldn't like any of you to find a bit of brain left stuck to your fingers afterwards.'

Tell your listeners that once the killer had dealt with the head, he turned his attention to smaller items of the torso. Pass round the carrots ('He took off the big toes') and the rubber gloves filled with soft earth and taped so that the earth cannot spill ('The hands are particularly interesting, and show the victim was probably quite young').

This could be the end of the story, but there is an optional extra: the beetroot. The beetroot is the heart, but of course beetroots stain, and you will

not want to stain the clothes of your listeners, or your tablecloth (which is why a plastic one is suggested). So if you use the beetroot, wrap it in a towel. Say:

'Lastly, the murderer removed the heart. Because some blood is not quite dried, I've wrapped it in a towel so that the blood will not stain your clothes. Be sure not to let the heart touch your clothes. When you've passed it on, wipe your hands on the baby wipe in front of you, as you wouldn't want to go home with blood on your hands.'

After the game
To prevent the possibility of your more sensitive guests having nightmares after the party, let them see the various body parts afterwards, when hopefully they will get the colour back into their cheeks and have a laugh about it all.

Chocolate race

Age range 7+
Number of players Any
Ideal for Introducing some energetic action into a children's party

This game could get a little rowdy, so you'll have to keep watch to see nothing is knocked over.

How to play
Put the knife, fork and chocolate on the plate and place it on a chair. Lay the hat, scarf and gloves by the side.

All the children sit in a circle. One has the dice in the shaker. Each player throws the dice in turn as the shaker is passed round the circle. As soon as the player throws a double, she rushes to the chair, puts on the hat, scarf and gloves, and begins to unwrap the chocolate. If she gets that far, she breaks off a piece of chocolate with a knife and fork and eats it.

However, while she's trying to do this, the rest are passing round the shaker, and as soon as another player throws a double, she shouts 'Double!' and rushes to the chair herself. The player trying to eat the chocolate must immediately put down the knife and fork and take off the hat, scarf and gloves, laying them on the

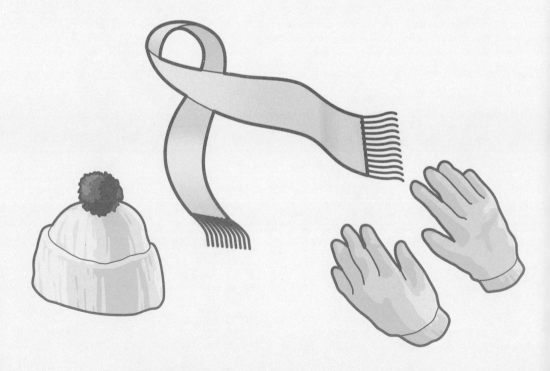

What you will need Two dice and a shaker, an old hat, scarf and pair of gloves, a knife, fork and plate, a largish bar of chocolate, a chair (preferably a wooden one without cushions – not an expensive one)

floor by the chair. She then rejoins the circle at the place where the player who called 'Double!' left it. The others are still taking turns to throw the dice.

Meanwhile, the player who threw the double is now at the chair, putting on the hat, scarf and gloves, and attempting to cut off a piece of chocolate for herself to eat.

The game ends when the chocolate is eaten, when the players are exhausted or when the chair is knocked over and chaos reigns.

> **! WARNING**
> It does not take long, perhaps only ten seconds or so, to throw a double with two dice, so it will often happen that a player will hardly have time to get on the hat, scarf and gloves before the next player is shouting 'Double'. It could therefore take some time before the chocolate is even unwrapped. You could get a scenario where one player is taking off the gear, another is putting it on, and a third is shouting 'Double!'
>
> If the game gets too prolonged, you could dispense with the gloves, which will make it easier for players to cut the chocolate.

Murder in the dark

Age range 8+
Number of players Any
Ideal for A party of mixed ages, best played in the evening when the lights can be switched off

This game is best played in a room large enough for people to move about in and it helps if the lights are out. The lights go on when the detective enters to solve the dastardly crime.

How to play

Once you know how many players are going to take part, you take that number of playing cards from the pack, ensuring that the cards you take include just one Ace and one Jack, the rest of the cards being ordinary cards from the 2 to the 10.

Shuffle the cards and ask each player to take one, not showing it to the others. Explain that the person who has the Jack is the murderer and the player who has the Ace is the detective.

Collect the cards and then ask the detective to reveal himself. Explain how the game works, which is as follows:

The detective goes out of the room and waits just outside the door. The lights in the room are switched off. The players are requested to move around the room (but if grandad and grandma are sitting in chairs they can stay there).

After a few seconds, the murderer (who is unknown to anybody but himself, remember) taps a victim on the shoulder and whispers 'I am the murderer and you are now dead'. The victim screams and lays down on the floor dead (or remains sitting comfortably in his or her armchair and feigns death).

When the scream is heard, all players must stand still where they are. Only the murderer is allowed to glide quickly away to another part of the room (if he or she wishes).

When the detective outside the door hears the scream, he counts to five (to allow the murderer to move) and enters the room, switching on the lights. He examines the corpse and begins to question anybody present in an effort to find the murderer.

During the questioning, only the murderer can tell a lie. All the others have to answer the detective truthfully.

Eventually the detective must decide who he thinks committed the murder and he must make an arrest by saying to the suspect 'I am arresting you for the dreadful murder of John Jones (naming the victim)'. If the detective is right, the killer confesses. If he is wrong, the right killer can now reveal himself, and if all agree, shuffle the cards and choose a new detective and murderer.

What you will need A pack of cards

The detective

The success of this game is largely due to the detective, who shouldn't just ask a perfunctory question or two and then make a guess. He can ask questions like: 'Why are you looking shifty?', 'Did you dislike the victim?', 'Do you think a man or a woman did it?', 'What was your motive in killing him?', 'Have you moved since the murder?' or 'You look a suspicious character ... was it you?'.

It is likely, of course, that many players will know who the murderer is (since the room might not be completely blacked out) so the detective is not allowed to ask questions like 'Where is the murderer standing now?'.

Squeak, piggy, squeak

Age range 6+
Number of players Any
Ideal for Children's birthday parties, when all are of similar age and are reasonably well acquainted with each other
What you will need A chair for each player, a cushion, a blindfold

This game promotes physical contact between the participants and brings them all into the game.

How to play

One child is chosen and is given a cushion and then blindfolded. The blindfolded child is turned round three times in the centre of the room while the other children sit on chairs around the room.

He then feels his way around the room until he finds somebody sitting on a chair. Putting the cushion on their lap and sitting down on it, he says 'Squeak, piggy, squeak'. The child on the chair has to squeak like a pig, and can be asked to repeat the squeak.

He must then guess whose lap he is sitting on. If he is right, that player becomes the guesser for the next round; if not, the guesser must find another player to sit upon and guess again.

When a new guesser is blindfolded, the children quickly change seats. If a guesser is wrong three times, then another guesser is chosen.

Age range 7+
Number of players 8+
Ideal for Livening up children's parties after
a quiet game or two
What you will need Four sturdy chairs, a
pack of cards

Royal court

**This is a shouting and dashing game. The
players need to be able to recognize the
four suits in a pack of cards.**

How to play

This game is best for 16 players. If you have this
number, place the four chairs in the four corners
of an imaginary square, facing inwards. The players
stand facing inwards on the imaginary lines
forming the square, with four players between
each chair.

Remove from a pack of cards the Ace, King,
Queen and Jack of each suit. Shuffle the 16
cards and spread them face-down on the floor in
the centre. On the command 'Go', each player
grabs a card. A player who picks up an Ace runs
to sit on a chair, calling out 'Ace of...', adding
whichever suit he has.

The other players whose cards are of the same
suit go to his chair. The holder of the King sits on
his knees with his feet on the floor, the holder of
the Queen sits on that player's knees and the
holder of the Jack on the third player's knees.

The first team to be seated correctly is
the winner.

For other numbers
If the number of players is divisible by three
but not four (so 9, 15, 18), you could
dispense with a suit and a chair. The number
sequence of cards to be used is also variable
to suit the number of players. Instead of Ace
to Jack, you could use Ace to Queen, 10 or 9.

⚠ WARNING
The host should let the players know
that care is to be taken when playing
this game as it could be painful for a
seven-year-old if he gets the Ace and three
heavy adults suddenly pile on top of him!

Put a cork in it

Age range 10+
Number of players Any (in teams)
Ideal for A funny interlude in a party that does not involve moving about
What you will need A cork (about 2.5 cm (1 in) high) from a wine bottle, a supply of small pieces of tissue paper, some questions

This is a game in which anyone above about ten years old can participate. It should present a few laughs.

Preparation
Write a number of questions on separate pieces of paper, about twice as many as there will be players. Cut out the same number of pieces of tissue paper, each about 5 cm (2 in) square.

How to play
Divide the players into two teams (not necessarily equal) and seat them in two groups. Hand the first player the cork and a piece of tissue paper, which she wraps round it. She then places the cork upright between her top and bottom teeth. Hand her one of the questions. She then has to read this out, with the cork in her mouth. She might have to repeat it, perhaps more than once.

The first player from either team who correctly answers the question wins a point for the team.

When the question is answered, the cork and (for hygiene purposes) a fresh piece of tissue paper are then handed to the first player from the second team, who reads out a second question. Continue until all members of both teams have read two questions. The team with the most points wins. Of course, an impartial referee (you) is needed to decide who correctly answered the question first.

Ten sample questions

* How old is dad?

* What was the artist Michaelangelo's first name?

* Who is president of the United States?

* What is butter made from?

* Who invented the telescope?

* What have I got in my mouth?

* How much did my haircut cost?

* Who is married to Catherine Zeta-Jones?

* In which year did the First World War start?

* Who is sitting north-west of me?

Though some of these are not particularly hard questions, they might be difficult to ask with a cork in your mouth.

Age range 10+
Number of players 4–6
Ideal for A party with older people who want a quiet game
What you will need An empty wine bottle and a supply of matches or cocktail sticks (say 10 for each player)

Piling up matches

This game tests the steadiness of the hand and becomes more tense as more and more matches become balanced on the bottle.

How to play

Stand an empty wine bottle (the cork can be used in the previous game) in the centre of the table. The narrower the neck of the bottle the better. The players sit around the table, each holding ten matches.

The first player balances a match across the mouth of the wine bottle. This is not difficult. The second player does the same, then the third, and so on. Soon a number of matches are balanced more or less precariously on the bottle and it becomes more and more difficult to add another without disturbing those that are there. Sooner or later somebody will knock some matches off. A player who knocks matches from the bottle to the table must take the spilt matches into his hand, and the turn passes to the next player. The player who manages to get rid of all his matches first is the winner. Since there is an advantage in going first, on a second game the first player should be the player on the left of the player who started the previous game, thus giving each player a chance to go first.

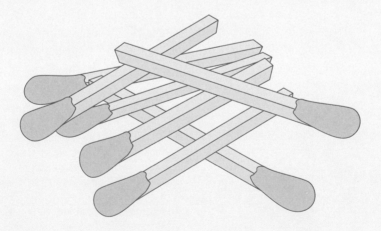

Fishing

Age range 7+
Number of players Any
Ideal for Family parties, as all can take part, although older players should be better than young children

This game requires some careful preparation, but it is one that children enjoy as it simulates fishing and allows them to show some dexterity. But be ready to intervene if lines get tangled up with each other.

Preparation
Make fishing rods by tying a piece of thin string about 90 cm (3 ft) long to one end of a cane. Attach a hook to the other end of the string.

Attach a short piece of thin string or thread to the cotton reels (as shown in the diagram). One

way of doing this could be to tie the string to diametrically opposite sides of a small rubber band, and slip the band over the cotton reel. At the bottom end of the reel write a small number from 1 to 5 (on 20 fish, say, have four of each number).

How to play
The cotton reels represent fish, and the number written on the bottom of the reel is the weight of the fish in pounds. The canes with hooks are, of course, the fishing rods.

Arrange the players on chairs in a circle so that a player's rod can reach far enough to dangle the hook at least to two-thirds of the way to the player sitting exactly opposite. The space inside the circle of chairs represents the pond. Stand the fish up around the centre of the pond so that all the hooks can reach them.

At the word 'Go', the players attempt to catch fish by manoeuvring their hooks underneath the cotton attached to the reels, and lifting them out of the pond.

Fishing goes on until all the fish are caught, or until a given time (say five minutes) has elapsed.

The number of fish should be about three times the number of players so as to give every player a chance of catching at least one or two fish.

The idea of giving the fish weights means that the player who catches most fish is not necessarily the winner. The winner is the player whose catch adds up to the most pounds. This gives the younger players a chance of winning.

What you will need Canes (of the type used by gardeners to support plants) of about 90–120 cm (3–4 ft) in length (one for each player), a ball of thin string, hooks of the sort that cups hang on or strong wire from which hooks can be made (one for each player), empty cotton reels (about three for each player), small elastic bands, a pen

Variation

As an alternative to writing numbers on the cotton reels you could write the name of a fish – pike, perch, tench, carp, dace, roach. Once the game ends, and all players have their catch, you can then announce values for each fish – a pike is worth 6 points, perch 5, tench 4, carp 3, dace 2, roach 1. The player with the highest count is the winner.

Dunking challenge

Age range 6+
Number of players Any
Ideal for Children's parties, including playful not-so-young children

Though this is a game that requires plenty of ingredients, preparation and some tidying up afterwards, it could provide a hysterical highlight to a children's party in the summer. Older people can join in, too, and earn some respect from the youngsters if they're sporting enough to get their faces covered in syrup or flour.

Preparation
A timekeeper will be required, as well as two or more adults to act as referees and keep the 'course' tidy and free of potential hazards (it could become slippery if too much water is spilt).

How to play
The course is set up. Mark a start line, and at about 1.8 m (6 ft) from this point place bowl 1. At intervals of 90 cm (3 ft), place bowls 2, 3 and 4.

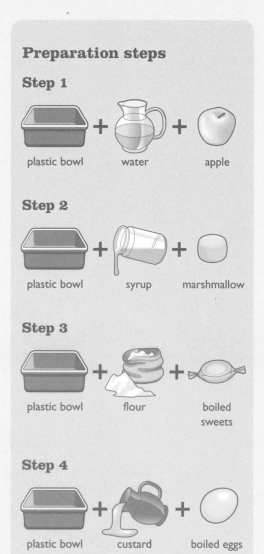

Preparation steps

Step 1

plastic bowl   water   apple

Step 2

plastic bowl   syrup   marshmallow

Step 3

plastic bowl   flour   boiled sweets

Step 4

plastic bowl   custard   boiled eggs

What you will need Four large plastic bowls, three bags of flour, three litres (five pints) of custard, two tins of syrup, clean water. An apple, a marshmallow, a boiled sweet and a peeled hard-boiled egg for each player. Protective clothing (a suit of overalls or a plastic mac), a stopwatch, towels and a supply of water for cleaning-up purposes

The first competitor dons the protective clothes if required and, on the command 'Go' (at which you start the stopwatch), runs to bowl 1 and kneels down. Without using his hands, which he keeps on the ground, he fishes out the apple with his teeth. Dropping the apple, he goes to bowl 2 and extracts similarly the marshmallow from the syrup. Putting that to one side, he extracts the boiled sweet from bowl 3, and then he extracts the egg from the custard in bowl 4. He runs back to the start line where his time is taken and noted down by the time-keeper.

The competitor is allowed two minutes at each bowl. If he fails to extract an item in two minutes, the time-keeper tells him to move on to the next bowl. Each 'missed' bowl incurs a two-minute time penalty.

After completing the course, the competitor is allowed to collect and keep his apple, his marshmallow, his boiled sweet and his egg, although it is unlikely he will really want his custard-flavoured egg. Water and a towel should be at hand so that he can clean himself up.

A referee tidies the course, puts a new apple, marshmallow, boiled sweet and egg into the respective bowls, and the next competitor is ready to start.

Variation

The game is perhaps better as a two-team game, but of course this requires another set of bowls and perhaps more syrup, flour and custard. When the first member of the team gets back to the start line, he touches the next member, who starts his run. As there is not therefore a gap between competitors, the referees must tidy and replenish the course as the race progresses. The time-keeper needs to set his watch when the first team completes the course and stop it when the second team completes. Provided the first finishers haven't cancelled out their winning margin by exceeding the second team's penalties, they are the winners.

WARNING

You should not press anybody to take part who is reluctant. Those with dentures shouldn't compete, nor those with smart clothes. Young girls might want to change out of their party dresses to compete. We suggest fresh apples and sweets for each competitor on hygiene grounds. Some people might still object to dunking their heads and mouths where others have gone before and their reservations should be respected.

What's the time, Mr Wolf?

Age range 3+
Number of players Any
Ideal for Young children's outdoor parties
What you will need A consoling sweet and maybe a piece of stretch plaster for any child knocked over in the chase

This is a traditional game which very young children enjoy. It is best if they are all of about the same size and speed.

How to play
One of the players is chosen to be Mr Wolf and the others are rabbits.

The rabbits line up at a start point and Mr Wolf starts with his back to them about 3 m (9 ft) ahead. The rabbits all call out 'What's the time, Mr Wolf?' Mr Wolf replies with whatever time he wishes, at the same time taking one pace forward. If he says 'Four o'clock', the rabbits make four little hops forwards, and again cry out, 'What's the time, Mr Wolf?' And so on.

As the rabbits make a little hop forward for each hour of Mr Wolf's times (and he could say 'Twelve o'clock') and Mr Wolf only takes one pace forward when he answers, the rabbits slowly get closer to Mr Wolf.

Eventually the question 'What's the time, Mr Wolf?' is answered by Mr Wolf as 'Dinner time', at which he turns and tries to catch a rabbit (by touching him), while all the rabbits run back to the start mark.

If Mr Wolf catches a rabbit, the rabbit becomes Mr Wolf for the next game.

Age range 4+
Number of players Any
Ideal for Children's birthday parties, where there is space for doing actions
What you will need The tact of a diplomat when Simon claims somebody moved, and the child in question denies it.

Simon says

Like What's the time, Mr Wolf? (see opposite), this is another traditional game, sometimes called Mrs Grundy says.

How to play
One child is chosen to be the leader, also known as Simon. He stands apart and gives the orders while the others arrange themselves facing him.

Simon orders the others to perform various actions by giving orders in the following manner: 'Simon says raise your arms above your head', 'Simon says touch your toes', 'Simon says stand on one foot' and 'Simon says fold your arms'. Simon himself also does the actions, and the others copy him and obey.

However, if Simon gives an order without prefixing it with 'Simon says', then the order must not be obeyed. So if Simon says 'Jump in the air', the others must stand still. If a child makes a mistake, he or she is out. Naturally, Simon tries to catch out as many as possible, sometimes by quickening up a succession of 'Simon says' and then suddenly leaving it out. Anyone who makes the slightest move leaves the game.

The last player left in is the winner and becomes Simon for the next round.

Simon says touch your toes

Simon says fold your arms

Jump in the air!

Corn flakes, anyone?

Age range 6+
Number of players Any
Ideal for Outdoor parties, such as barbecues

This is a game that all ages can play, though possibly uniquely in this book, the smaller and younger you are the better you might be at it. In fact, you might have three or four separate competitions, dividing your players up into classes. For example: under–9 (nursery class), 9–14 (junior class), 15–30 (senior class), 30+ (decrepit class).

Preparation
Take a large-size cereal box (or boxes, if you are going to have classes of entrant), throw away the inside packet and cut off the flaps at the top.

How to play
This is an extremely simple game in principle, but not so simple in practice.

Stand the box up on a nice soft level patch of grass – level so that the box will stand up, soft because standing is probably more than some of the competitors will be able to do.

Line up your competitors and ask the first to step forward and pick up the box. There are only two restrictions: she must do it with her teeth, and only her feet may touch the ground. In other words, the player has to bend over (ouch) and bring her mouth down to the box. As is frequently said, 'Don't try this at home.' Not if the best days of your youth are past, anyway!

All players attempt this in turn, and those who succeed stand to one side for the second round (oh yes!) while those whose backs give out or who topple over in the attempt are relegated.

Now you perform the unkindest cut of all. Cut about 2.5 cm (1 in) from the top of the box and let all those who succeeded try again. Once again, with luck, there will be a toppler or two to provide some unsympathetic laughter.

As you will have guessed, this continues round by round with you cutting 2.5 cm (1 in) from the box each round (you might be surprised at how small the box gets) until only one player is left – she or he of the most supple limbs and the best balance is the winner.

This is a game that will make older people feel their age, but they should be glad to discover that the phrase 'flexible friends' can mean something more than those cards they keep in their wallets and purses.

What you will need Three or four empty
cereal boxes, scissors

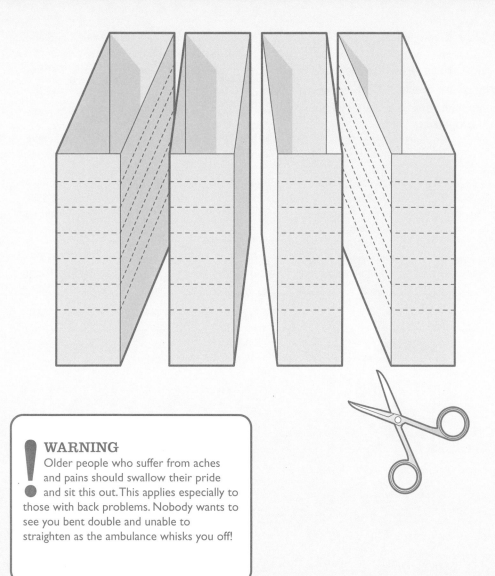

! **WARNING**
   Older people who suffer from aches
   and pains should swallow their pride
   and sit this out. This applies especially to
   those with back problems. Nobody wants to
   see you bent double and unable to
   straighten as the ambulance whisks you off!

Broken bottle

Age range 10+
Number of players Any
Ideal for Outdoor parties where there is reasonable space to throw a ball
What you will need A tennis ball or a similar soft ball, plus a readiness to settle arguments as to whether a catch was a fair one or not

This is a catching game where every missed catch proves costly – a player who misses too many will find himself having to use one hand only, or making catches on his knees, until eventually he is out altogether.

How to play

Players form a circle, with one holding the ball, and proceed to throw the ball to each other. It is best if the ball is thrown across the circle rather than to someone close by. It is suggested that a rule be applied that a player must throw the ball to the player standing to the right of the one from whom he received it. In this way the ball

should go round and round the circle. In every case the thrower should call out the name of the player he is throwing to, thus preventing two players trying to make the same catch.

To start, everybody catches the ball with both hands. However, as soon as a player misses a catch, he must put his left hand behind his back, and thereafter use his right hand only. If he misses a second catch, he must put his right hand behind his back and use his left hand only. On his third miss, a player must go down on one knee, but may use both hands again. If he misses again, he must go down on both knees.

If a player misses a fifth catch, he must stay down on both knees but put his left hand behind him and use his right only.

His sixth miss is the last that will be allowed him. He stays kneeling on both knees but must now catch with his left hand only, holding his right behind his back. Another miss and he is out.

Play continues as more and more drop out until only one player is left – the winner.

Occasionally, a throw will be so bad that it would be unreasonable to expect the catcher to catch it, especially if he is kneeling and cannot move towards the ball. In such cases those players still in the game may deem it an unfair throw, and the player who failed to catch the ball is not penalized, remaining in the game.

Age range 6–8
Number of players 6+
Ideal for Outdoor birthday parties,
particularly for young girls, since the theme
is witches
What you will need A good-sized lawn,
and if you wish to make it realistic, two or
three black hats, pointed if possible, and two
or three brooms

Wicked
witches

**This is a game in which two or three
children play witches. It entails a good
deal of chasing and probably a certain
amount of screaming.**

Preparation
The witches (two or three according to the
number of players) will look and feel more
wicked if they have black hats. If you are handy
enough to make cones from cardboard and paint
them black, that would be excellent. If not, any
old black hats from an adult's wardrobe would
do nicely.

How to play
If there are ten or fewer players, two witches
would be sufficient – more than ten players
perhaps require three witches.

The witches are chosen and they put on their
hats and take their broomsticks and go and hide
in a corner of the garden. If there is nowhere

where they can actually hide, it doesn't matter –
they can stand in a corner huddled together and
whispering to themselves.

The other children are asked to dance and skip
about the lawn, knowing that sooner or later the
witches will be coming to get them. So the daring
children skip as close to the witches as they dare.

After a few seconds the witches decide to strike,
and without warning they come shrieking and
yelling from their corner trying to touch the
other players. When a witch touches a player
she calls 'Tag' and that player is turned to stone
and must immediately stand still till the end of
the game.

The witches can touch the players only by hand
and must always take care not to touch them
with the broomsticks, which doesn't count.

The game ends when all the players have been
tagged and all is still. The last two or three tagged
then become the witches for the next game and
take over the hats and broomsticks and huddle
away in the corner.

> **! WARNING**
> It does happen that children running
> about with broomsticks run the risk of
> causing accidents by tripping up other
> children or inadvertently hitting them with
> their broomsticks. If you feel this is a danger,
> or if some children appear reckless with
> their broomsticks, you should put them
> away and play the game without.

French cricket

Age range 10+
Number of players Any
Ideal for Outdoor parties where there is a good amount of space, especially if the guests like cricket
What you will need A child's baseball bat or tennis racquet and a tennis ball or similar soft ball

This is a game where it is essential that the ball is a soft one, as part of the game is to throw it to hit the batsman's legs.

How to play

One player is the batsman and has the bat. One of the other players, who are fielders and surround the batsman at a distance of about 10 m (33 ft), has the ball. He throws the ball at the batsman's legs, below the knee. If he hits, the batsman is out, but the batsman protects himself with the bat and is permitted to knock the ball away (though not too hard).

If the batsman hits the ball, the nearest fielder collects it and has a shy at the batsman's legs. The batsman is permitted to turn to face the thrower. This makes it easier for him to protect himself, so putting him at an advantage.

If, however, the batsman misses the ball, the ball is still fielded by the nearest player to where it goes, who has the next throw. This time, though, by virtue of having missed the ball, the batsman cannot turn to face the fielder but must remain facing the way he was. He may still turn his head towards the fielder, of course, but it makes it more difficult to protect his legs if the ball is coming from behind him.

When a fielder hits the batsman below the knees, he becomes the batsman, and the batsman becomes a fielder.

Charlie Chaplin relay

Age range 8+
Number of players Any (in teams)
Ideal for An outdoor family party of all ages
What you will need Two balloons, two books or small cushions, two walking sticks, two cones or buckets

Young children might not have heard of Charlie Chaplin, but the Charlie Chaplin relay is good fun nevertheless and even grandad can join in.

How to play

Two teams are selected. A string is placed on the lawn for a start line. Two upturned buckets or traffic cones are placed at a distance of about 6 m (20 ft), with 3 m (10 ft) between them.

The first player to go in each team puts a balloon between his knees, a book or cushion on his head and takes a walking stick in his hand.

On the command 'Go', the first players set off waddling down the course, keeping the balloon between their knees, balancing the book or cushion, and twirling the stick à la Charlie

Chaplin. They round their bucket or cone and return to the start line, whereupon the next player takes over the balloon, book and cane and sets off.

If the balloon or book is dropped, the player stops and replaces it. If the balloon is burst, the team is disqualified and loses.

The first team to complete the course wins. Have some extra balloons in reserve for accidents and re-runs.

Sinking ship

Age range 6+
Number of players Any (in teams)
Ideal for An outdoor family party of all ages
What you will need A large bowl, a slightly smaller one, a small plastic cup

This is a game where all the family can join in, but its main attraction is to allow the young to play with water.

Preparation
Nearly fill the large bowl with water. Float the smaller bowl on the surface.

How to play
Form the players into two equal teams and line each team up on opposite sides of the bowl. One player from team A is given the plastic cup and with this she takes as much water as she wants from the large bowl (but not less than half a cup full) and pours it into the smaller bowl; she then retires to the back of her team's line.

The first player from team B then takes the plastic cup and does the same. In alternate turns each member of the two teams pours some water from the large bowl into the smaller one until the smaller bowl is on the point of sinking, and players have to be more and more careful in pouring in the water.

Eventually a player pours into the smaller bowl enough water to make it sink. That player then leaves the game and the smaller bowl is emptied and set afloat again; players continue to fill it, one from each team alternately. One player is eliminated each time the bowl sinks.

Finally, all of one team is eliminated, and the other team wins.

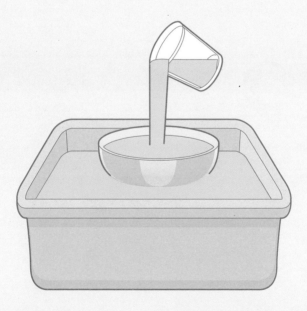

Age range 6+
Number of players 4+
Ideal for Large parties of children of the same age, such as birthday parties
What you will need The judgement of Solomon, as you will be asked to settle who won a close race

Tapping hands

This is a running game, which might lead to a scramble or two. Because of this, it is a good idea for an adult or two to act as referee.

How to play

All the players except one form a large circle. There could be, if space allows, about 1.8 m (6 ft) between them, so that anybody running round the edge of a circle of 12 children would have to run about 30 m (100 ft).

The children face inwards and clasp their hands behind their backs. The odd player (who can volunteer or be selected by the referee) is the first tapper. She runs round the circle until at any point she taps the hands of one of the players in the circle.

The tapper continues running, while the player tapped must run round the circle in the opposite direction. The two race to get back to the space created in the circle, the first there filling the space. If the tapper loses, she continues running and taps another player. If the tapper wins, the loser continues running and becomes the tapper.

To avoid a collision, it should be agreed that when the two runners pass, the tapper (who, after all gets a start) must run round the outside of the player tapped. To give everybody a chance to play, the tapper cannot tap a player she has already raced against.

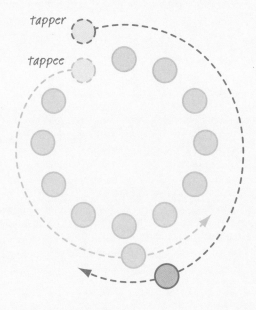

tapper

tappee

Christmas pudding

Age range 8–12
Number of players Any even number
Ideal for A children's party, when a boisterous game is needed
What you will need A recipe for a Christmas pudding which can be adapted

This game should be ideal for Christmas, but as a certain amount of jostling is possible, it is suggested as an outside game for the summer.

Preparation

You need a list of ingredients for a Christmas pudding, one ingredient for each child playing. Maybe you could write out your own recipe, which need not be viable (after all, you are not going to make the pudding). Ideally, you want one that mentions each ingredient twice (maybe one or two of them three times). You can make it easier for yourself by rewriting an existing recipe.

How to play

The children sit on the ground in two rows facing each other. Their legs are stretched out before them with their feet touching the feet of the player opposite. It is best if this game is played barefoot. There should be 1 m (3 ft) between the children to allow a space between the pairs of touching legs. As the children are going to run down the line between the facing rows there must be room for them to place their feet without stepping on the sitting children's legs.

Give each child the name of an ingredient in the Christmas pudding recipe. The child must remember this ingredient.

You explain that you are going to read out the recipe and that every time their ingredient is mentioned, they must run behind their row and, on reaching the end, should run down the middle of the two rows – jumping over the legs as they go – to the other end of the rows. They then run back behind their own row to reoccupy their original place and sit with their legs in the middle as before.

You must ensure that the children know which end of the rows to run to first because a collision between two children vaulting legs from opposite directions could cause tears before bedtime. Keep your eye on the game and do not read the recipe too fast – you do not want three or four children running past the outstretched legs at the same time.

The fun comes when two or three ingredients are read at once, or when a player, having run through the legs, sits down again only to hear his ingredient read out again.

Age range 8–12
Number of players Up to 16
Ideal for Parties for children where perhaps
there are an equal number of boys and girls
What you will need A washing line at an
appropriate height for the children to hang
clothes on, 12 handkerchiefs and 24 clothes
pegs (or 18 hankies and 36 clothes pegs if
your supplies stretch so far), and two lengths
of string to mark out the start lines

Hanging out the washing

**Most children will be aware of the need
to hang washing out to dry. In this game
they get to do it themselves.**

Preparation
Erect a clothes line as specified and fix on the
grass with lengths of string two start lines, one
each side of the clothes line about 4 m (13 ft)
from the clothes line.

How to play
First of all, arrange your children in pairs so that
they form teams of two, ideally with a boy and a
girl in each team, but if there are more boys than
girls, or vice-versa, it doesn't matter – you will
just have to have some unisex teams.

Each team requires 6 hankies and 12 pegs, so if
you have 12 hankies and 24 pegs available, you
will have to run a number of heats between two
teams, the winning team going on to the next
round each time. Obviously if you have 18
hankies and 36 pegs, three teams can compete
per race and with one going through each time
you will get to the final quicker.

Suppose two teams are competing. The two boys
stand one side of the clothes line (having half the
clothes line each) and their partners the opposite
side facing them. All stand behind the starting
lines you've marked out, each boy holding 12 pegs
and each girl 6 hankies. On the command 'Go', all
run to the line, where the partners meet each
other. The girl takes one peg at a time from the
boy, and pegs up the hankies, two pegs to each
hankie. When they are all pegged up (and not
before), the boy then unpegs them and passes the

pegs, one at a time as he does so, to the girl, while
keeping the hankies. When all are unpegged, the
boy with the pegs and the girl with the hankies
run back to their marks. The team to get both
boy and girl back to their marks first are the
winners, and go through to the next round.
Eventually there will be a final, and the overall
champion team emerges.

Several umpires
You will need at least two or three umpires,
one for each team, to ensure that the rules
are followed and the hankies are correctly
hung up before they are taken down again,
and in case of argument somebody must
judge which of the sides had both their
players back to the starting line first.

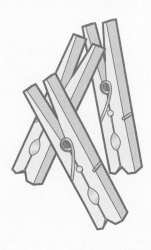

Three-legged race

Age range 5–8
Number of players Any even number (in teams)
Ideal for Outdoor parties
What you will need One length of soft, thick material such as a pillow case or stockings (for each pair of players to tie a leg of one player to the leg of her partner), a length of rope to mark out the course

This popular race, a fixture on certain party sports days, is recommended to be run outside. This is because there are likely to be falls, and the coming together of young heads and old furniture is unlikely to benefit either.

How to play

The race is run in pairs, so the first task is to arrange the pairs. A course of about 15–20 m (49–66 ft) is about right.

A start and finish line are marked on the grass with string. Each pair is tied together just above the ankles, the right leg of one partner being tied to the left leg of the other. Be careful not to tie the legs so tightly that the rope will hurt, and try not to leave loose ends which might be tripped over.

Pairs line up behind the start line and, on the command 'Go', race to the finish line. Any fallers may get up and continue, but if the rope comes undone, the team must leave the race. The first pair to the finish line wins.

Age range 5–8
Number of players Any
Ideal for A bit of fun at children's parties
What you will need A sack (could be a duvet cover or sleeping bag) for each player (plastic bin liners, although more readily available, would be less satisfactory as they would probably tear), string for marking out the course

Sack race

This is a traditional race for outdoor children's parties. It usually provides a few tumbles and lots of laughs, but nobody should hurt themselves if the ground is grassy.

How to play
Mark out a course by stretching lengths of string for start and finish lines, about 15–20 m (49–66 ft) apart.

Each runner steps into her sack, gathers it round her waist and holds it up – she must not let it fall round her ankles during the race. Any fallers can get up and continue.

Sack shortage
If you have, say, only four sacks and 16 children, organize heats. Four heats of four runners would suffice, with the first two in each heat going into two semi-finals, where the first two in each race meet in a final.

On the command 'Go', the runners jump or bounce to the finish line, the first to arrive being the winner.

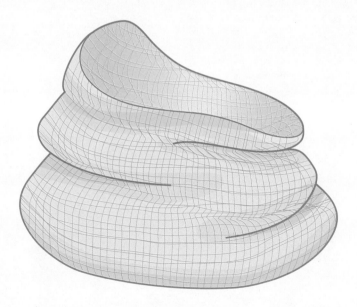

Egg and spoon race

Age range 6–10
Number of players Any
Ideal for Outdoor children's parties
What you will need A dessert spoon and a hard-boiled egg (or a golf ball) for each competitor, string to mark out a course

This is a traditional game. If you have more children than you can prepare hard-boiled eggs for, or are not a golfer, you can find a champion by organizing heats as mentioned on page 93 for the Sack race, or you could run the race as a relay, needing only one egg and spoon for each team. Table-tennis balls are not a good substitute for eggs, as they are too light, especially in a wind.

Variation
To make it slightly harder and to introduce a slight element of dressing-up into proceedings, each child could be given an adult's glove, into which they must put both their hands and hold the spoon two-handed through the glove. This will make it a little more awkward for them, especially if they drop the egg and have to pick it up again.

How to play
Use a 15–20 m (49–66 ft) course, marked out by string at the start and finish lines. Each runner balances an egg in his spoon, and on the command 'Go' must race from the start to the finish line. The eggs must not be touched by hand. If they fall out of the spoons, the runner must stop, and can pick up the egg, but must have it safely in the spoon before beginning to run again. The first to cross the finish line wins.

Age range 8+
Number of players Any (in teams)
Ideal for Children's parties
What you will need A soft surface such as grass and a careful eye to see that no children are embarrassed or hurt by being pushed on their faces

Wheelbarrow race

This is another traditional children's race game. It does not need any special equipment, but is not suitable for children under about eight years old, as a certain strength and discretion is required.

How to play

The contestants pair off into teams of two, if possible a boy and girl in each. Line up the pairs on a 15–20 m (49–66 ft) track.

One member of each pair is the wheelbarrow. He gets down on hands and knees behind the start line. On the command 'Ready', his partner, the wheelbarrow pusher, picks up his legs by the ankles, one in each hand. On the command 'Go', the pair set off for the finish line, the wheelbarrow 'walking' on his hands, and the pusher walking behind. The first pair to arrive at the finish wins.

Variation

At the finish, the wheelbarrow and the pusher could change places and race back. If you like, you can make the two races into one continuous race, the winning pair being that which gets back to the start line first.

WARNING
There is a tendency for the 'pusher' to take his title too literally, and actually to push, which results in the 'wheelbarrow' being unable to keep going fast enough, and falling on his face, or at least his stomach. An adult should be on hand to watch out for this.

Age range 5+
Number of players Any even number
(in teams)
Ideal for An outdoor family party for
all ages
What you will need Two plates,
five potatoes and one dessert spoon for
each team

Potato race

**This is a fun relay race, where fortunes
can change quickly, especially if one or
two dodgy grandads take part.**

How to Play

Sort the players into two equal teams. Using the
15–20 m (49–66 ft) course suggested for the
previous race games, set an empty plate at the
start line for each team and, similarly, at the finish
line a plate containing five potatoes.

The first runner for each team is given a dessert
spoon. On the command 'Go', she must run to
the finish line, pick up a potato with her spoon
(hands must never be used to touch the potatoes
in this game) and run back to the start line,
where she deposits it on the empty plate. She

then runs back four more times, each time
bringing back one potato in the same way. If a
potato is dropped, either in running or
transferring it onto the plate, it must be picked up
with the spoon, not the hands.

When all the potatoes are safely on the plate at
the start line, the next runner takes the spoon,
picks up a potato and transfers it back to the
plate at the finish line. She then returns and
transfers the other potatoes. When she has
transported all five potatoes, she hands the spoon
to the third runner, who brings them back again
and so on.

The first team to have all its runners back behind
the start line with all the potatoes on the correct
plate is the winner.

Age range 8+
Number of players 8+ (in teams)
Ideal for A bit of fun with balloons
What you will need Two balloons (plus spares in case of accidents), a blindfold for each player

Blind tunnel race

This is a game that is played between two teams and, to avoid possible embarrassment, it might be best to have a team of boys versus a team of girls. The fun in this game comes when a blindfolded team loses control of the balloon, and its straight line begins to waver. Ensure that there is at least 90 cm (3 ft) between each player so that they must reach for the balloon and hopefully get into a muddle.

How to play

Each team forms a line with one player behind another. Each player is blindfolded, and stands with legs apart. The first player in each team is given a balloon. If the teams are of mixed sex, they can be called Team A and Team B, if they are of the same sex, Girls and Boys. The object is to pass the balloon backwards through the legs from front to back. As soon as the last player of the team has the balloon safely in hand, he or she shouts 'About turn', announcing the name of the team – for example, 'About turn, Girls' – at which each member of the team must turn around 180 degrees, including the player who calls out.

The balloon is then passed back between the legs of each player as before, and when it reaches the end so that it is back with the player who started with it, he or she raises it high, shouting 'Boys win' or 'Girls win' or whatever the team name is.

Dressing-up relay

Age range 8–12
Number of players 8+ (two teams)
Ideal for A silly relay item in a party where older children are in the majority
What you will need Two plastic bowls and two sets of old clothes (a hat, skirt, jacket, trousers, scarf, gloves, socks), string for a start line

This is an exciting, if somewhat silly, game. Each set of clothes must have the same items, and there should be as many items as there are players on a team.

How to play

Pick two teams, equal in number, speed and strength. Lay a line of string at one end of the course as a start point, and place the two bowls with the clothing items about 20 m (66 ft) away. Remember there must be an item of clothing for each player.

At the word 'Go', the first player from each team runs to his bowl and puts on one item of clothing (say, the hat). He runs back to the start line, takes off the hat and hands it to the second runner, who puts it on and races back to the bowl. She adds a second item of clothing (say, the scarf). She runs back to the start line, takes them both off, hands them to the third runner, who puts them on, runs to the bowl and puts on a third item. He runs back to the fourth runner and so on.

The last runner should come running back to the start line wearing all the clothes. The bowl will be empty. It is best if the older runners go last, as they have more to do.

The first team to complete the course with a fully clothed player wins.

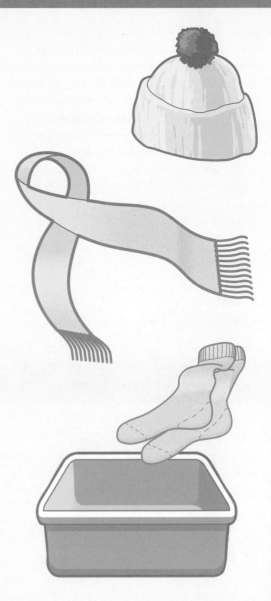

Age range 10+
Number of players Any even number
Ideal for An outdoor party of older
children (who can catch)
What you will need Two balls or quoits,
two canes, string

Spry

**This is a catching game in which adults
can play with older children. The ideal
amount of players for this game is 12.**

How to play

Select two teams. The two team leaders stand
almost back to back with their teams facing them
in a line about 3.7 m (12 ft) away. There should be
1.8 m (6 ft) between each team member. Canes
could be laid on the ground to mark out the
leaders' position, and string for the teams'
positions. The illustration shows the layout for six
players per team.

The leader starts with the ball. He throws it to

player 1, who returns it, then players 2, 3, 4, who
return it. Player 5, however, instead of returning
the ball, runs to the centre and becomes leader,
throwing it to the other players in turn except
the original player 4, who himself becomes leader.
The other players then shift to the left.

The same routine is repeated. When the original
leader has reached position 5, and the ball is
thrown to her, she runs with it to the leader's
position, while all the players shift to the left, so
that all are in their original starting positions. The
first team to achieve this wins.

If a ball is dropped, the ball has to be returned to
the player who threw it, and be re-thrown.

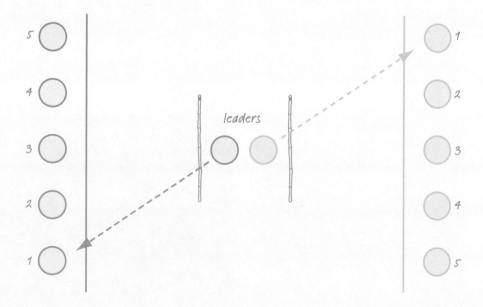

Stepping stones

Age range 6+
Number of players Any (in teams)
Ideal for Children's birthday parties, where there are a number of children of more or less equal ages

Like all racing games, this can be a race between individuals, or a relay between teams. It is probably best to make it a team race as you will not need as many stepping stones.

Preparation

The ideal stepping stones could be pieces of wood, as if cut from a plank or shelf, of about 15 x 15 cm (6 x 6 in). Pieces of cardboard of a similar size would do. Unless you are going to race on a wet surface, sheets of newspaper would suffice. Shoeboxes, or shoebox lids, would be fine, but they must be big enough for the feet of the competitors to fit inside. Plastic hoops of the same size would also do.

How to play

Form two or more equal teams, according to the number of players. Lay lengths of string to mark out a start and finish line, about 15 m (49 ft) apart. Half of each team should be at the start line, and half at the finish line. With an odd number in the team, the extra player should be at the start line. Hand the first player of each team a pair of stepping stones.

The race begins with the first player throwing down a stepping stone a short distance in front of her. She then steps on this with one foot, and throws down the other stepping stone just in

front of this, on which she places her second foot. She must then lift her first foot from the stepping stone, and balancing on her second foot must pick up the first stepping stone, place that down in front of her, and put her foot on that. In this manner she progresses to the finish line. At no time can any part of her body touch the ground. If she overbalances or in any way touches the ground, she must take the stepping stones back to the beginning of the course and start again.

The first player completes the course when she throws one stepping stone over the finish line, and with her foot on it picks up the other stepping stone. She then hands the stepping stone to the waiting second player, and he makes his way back to the start line in the same manner, where the third player takes over, and so on. The first team to have all members complete the course wins.

A touch of chivalry

If there were an even number of players in a team, you could split the teams into pairs (ideally boy/girl). The pair should go down the course together, with the girl acting, perhaps, as a queen or princess and stepping on the stones, while the boy plays an old-fashioned gentleman, picking up the stepping stone behind her and with a bow placing it in front of her for the next step.

What you will need Two stepping stones
(see below) for each team, string

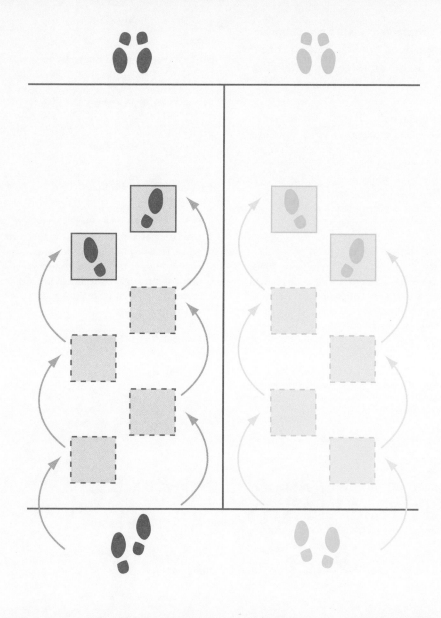

Assault course

Age range 6+
Number of players Any
Ideal for Parties with children of similar age, such as a birthday party

This amusing game will have children running around to their hearts' content. You can be imaginative when thinking of elements to add to the course.

Preparation

Set up an assault course, with string stretched across the ground to mark a start line. The same line can serve as the finish line if you can organize a circular course which beings the runner back to the starting point. Each point on the course is marked with a number written on a piece of card placed on the ground by the obstacle.

How to play

Before the start, the course must be explained to all runners so that they know what to do. There must be a timekeeper with a watch to take and record each runner's time, so that a winner can be announced. Water and a towel should be handy if the runner has to scrabble through a bowl of earth.

There should be a couple of adults marshalling the course to replace every item ready for the next player.

Team game

You could divide your runners into teams of three or four. The first runner of the team, on passing the finish line, touches the second who begins to run. Rather than individual times, you then have to record team times.

Suggested obstacles

Point 1 An obstacle that has to be jumped over, such as a stack of three cardboard boxes standing one upon the other. If the runner knocks them over, he must rebuild them and try again, but if he knocks them down three times he is allowed to continue to the next point.

Point 2 A sack. The runner takes off his shoes, climbs into the sack and bumps along to Point 3.

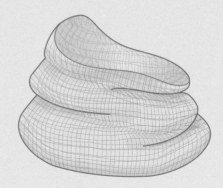

What you will need Objects to form an assault course. Suggestions are included in the description below, but you can invent your own, according to what you have to hand. Also, a stopwatch, a length of string and pieces of card

Point 3 An old shirt, an old sweater and a hat. The runner puts on the three items and bumps back in the sack to Point 2, where he leaves the sack and puts on his shoes. He returns to Point 3, where he takes off the old shirt, sweater and hat, leaving them there to run to Point 4.

Point 4 A bowl of water containing three hard-boiled eggs, next to which is a dessert spoon. The runner must fish an egg out of the bowl with the dessert spoon and run to Point 5.

Point 5 A plate. The egg must be placed carefully on the plate, and the runner has to go back to Point 4 twice more to fetch the other eggs in the same way. When all three are safely on the plate (any dropped at any time must be picked up with the spoon) he lays the spoon by the plate and runs to Point 6.

Point 6 A skipping rope and a large adult's hat. He must put on the hat (which might fall over his eyes), take the skipping rope and skip ten times without the hat falling off (if it does, he must put it back on and start his ten skips again). Having done this, he leaves the hat and skipping rope and runs to Point 7.

Point 7 A bowl of sand or earth with a coin buried in it. The runner must find the coin (without spilling the sand or earth out of the bowl) and place it beside the bowl. He then runs back to and over the start line.

Number plates

Age range 6+
Number of players 2–4
Ideal for Keeping passengers occupied on long car journeys
What you will need To show support and interest during those periods when the game seems to stall

This is a cooperative game to keep passengers alert and interested on a long journey. If everyone works together, there is shared satisfaction if you succeed.

How to play

The object is to work through the alphabet from A to Z by mentally ticking off the letters as they are spotted on car number plates. Only the letters that appear at either end of the whole number plate count, and they must be spotted in the correct order. Therefore, the first thing to find is a car with an A at the beginning or end of its number plate. When A has been found, you then search for B.

The letters must be spotted in the correct sequence. If you are looking for M and you see N, you cannot keep the N 'in reserve' and count M and N when you later see M. It can be frustrating, but it's better than the perpetual 'Are we nearly there yet?' every five minutes.

Variations

If you want a quicker game, you can allow any letter in the car number plate to be eligible, not just those at each end. In this case, if you are looking for C, for example, and a car number plate has C and D, you count both.

Age range 9–12
Number of players 2–4
Ideal for Passing a bit of time on long car journeys
What you will need A willingness to smooth over arguments about whether somebody has taken too long, for example

Next letter

This is a simple, competitive game where players get knocked out if they cannot go.

How to play

A subject is chosen – countries, for example. The first player must name a country beginning with the letter A. The next player names a country beginning with B, and so on down the alphabet, the turn going round from player to player. A player who cannot produce a country beginning with the appropriate letter within, say, five seconds, is eliminated, and the last player remaining is the winner.

Suggested subjects
* Countries
* Towns
* Animals
* Football teams
* Boys' names
* Girls' names
* Capital cities
* Recording artists
* Parts of the body
* Sportsmen's surnames
* Celebrities' surnames

The postman's dog

Age range 9–12
Number of players 2–4
Ideal for Taking the minds of 9- to 12-year-olds off a tedious journey
What you will need To provide encouragement by praising good efforts

This is a competitive game, where young passengers might get eliminated soonest. The last surviving player is the winner.

How to play

Each player has to describe and name the postman's dog, the first with words beginning with A, the second B and so on. If a player cannot do it in within, say, five seconds, then he or she drops out.

For example, the first player could say 'The postman's dog is an angry dog and its name is Arthur'. The second player has B, and might say 'The postman's dog is a brown dog and its name is Bruno'. And so on. The letter X can be omitted.

Variation

Each player has to provide a description and a name for each letter. The youngest player goes first each time. With three players, the first dog could be angry, awkward and agile and its name Arthur, Algy and Albert. You might decide to leave out the more difficult letters Q and Z as well as X.

I'll take my Auntie Pam's dog

Age range 8+
Number of players 2–4
Ideal for Otherwise boring car journeys
What you will need A readiness to get involved and to suggest the end-of-sentence requirements for successive games

This is a competitive game, but not to be taken too seriously. It's object, after all, is to provide some entertainment on a long car journey, so the more weird and wonderful items players can dream up to take to the cinema the more laughs there will be.

How to play

This is another game where players are eliminated if they do not come up with a correct item quickly enough when it is their turn.

Each player in turn must supply an end to the sentence: 'Tonight I'm going to the cinema, and I'm taking my...'. The missing word or words must agree to a formula. For example, they could be a word beginning with a certain letter. If it were W, successive players could take a wig, water pistol, watch or wheelbarrow. The item taken need not be relevant, so players can dream up the funniest items they like.

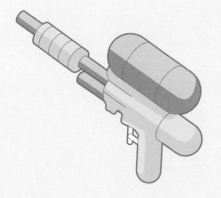

The end-of-sentence requirement could be any two-word item, so players could take a mobile phone, Wellington boots, toilet paper and so on.

You could make it quite difficult (where the items taken might get outlandish) such as stipulating the sentence must end with a 'three-word item beginning with A'. Then you could say 'Tonight I'm going to the cinema and I'm taking my Auntie Pam's dog' or 'my anti-tetanus pills' or 'my arty suede shoes'.

Other requirements could be you must take an item beginning with the last letter of the previous player's item, so the sequence might go: harp, pyjamas, socks, saucepan, newspaper, rabbit, teeth, hairspray, yogurt and so on.

Or the items taken must be items of six letters, so my canary, eyelid, carrot, kitten and so on.

A player failing to provide a suitable sentence within ten seconds on his turn is eliminated.

Food store

Age range 7+
Number of players 2–4
Ideal for Keeping the back-seat passengers occupied when travelling, especially if there's nothing much to see through the window
What you will need A willingness to join in if interest seems to be waning

This is a game that can be played by any number at any time, but is suitable for this specialized travelling use. It is a sort of I spy (see page 43) of the mind.

How to play

The player who agrees to start says 'My father runs a food store and in it he sells something beginning with...'. And she names the first letter of the item she is thinking of. The other players then try to guess what the item is. For instance, if the letter was P, the item might be potatoes, plums, pies or peppermints.

The first to guess what the item is then becomes the one whose father runs the shop, and sets a puzzle for the others. When the subject of food seems exhausted, the father's shop could become a newsagent.

Variation

Players take turns to make the statement 'My father runs a food store...'. The first player must think of something beginning with A, and end the sentence accordingly. When the item is guessed, the next player must make the statement and the object must begin with B. And so on. Each player on their turn must be given a minute or two to think of an object beginning with the appropriate letter. By agreement, and if you get that far, the letters Q, X and Z can be omitted.

Age range 7+
Number of players 2–4
Ideal for Providing entertainment for
tedious journeys
What you will need A certain amount of
patience as you listen to lists endlessly
repeated; remember – it's keeping them
occupied

One omelette

This game is another that can actually be
played at a party with any number of
players, but since it requires nothing but
imagination it is particularly suitable for
whiling away the time sitting in the car.

One Omelette

How to play

Players in this game take turns to name objects
according to the rules of the game, and a player
who fails is eliminated.

The first player must name an object beginning
with the letter O, as O is the first letter of 'One'.
She might say 'One omelette'. Each player in turn
repeats 'One Omelette', including the first player
to say it. The second player now says 'One
omelette and two...', adding something beginning
with T, for 'Two'. He might say 'One omelette and
two toffees'. All in turn repeat this until the third
player comes in again, and she says 'One
omelette, two toffees and three...'. And so on.

Two Toffees

Notice that 'Three' also begins with T, so two
things beginning with T get into the list. Also, of
course, 'Four' and 'Five' each start with F, 'Six' and
'Seven' with S, and when 'Ten' is reached, a third
item beginning with T gets into the list.

Players are eliminated less because they cannot
think of an item beginning with the appropriate
letter but because they forget the order of the
items already listed. Any hesitation and a player
automatically is out.

Ending the game

It is unlikely that this game will last beyond
the 20s and 30s because every new object
(20 altogether) must begin with the letter T,
and it will be difficult for players to
remember which object beginning with T
fitted, for example, 'twenty-three' and which
fitted 'twenty-four'. In fact by then the game
is likely to disintegrate in argument, and you
must gently suggest a new one.

I love my love

Age range 8+
Number of players 2–4
Ideal for Car journeys, when impatience creeps in among the younger travellers
What you will need The ability to join in occasionally to keep things going

In this game, players have a chance to show off a little by using rather outlandish words.

How to play

Players in turn take a successive letter of the alphabet and complete the following sentence by filling in the spaces with a name, an adjective, a place name and a present, all beginning with the relevant letter.

The first player starts with the letter A and says 'I love my love with an A, because her name is A..., she is a..., she comes from A... and I shall give her a...'.

The second player then does the same with the letter B, and so on. Any player who cannot complete the sentence on his letter leaves the game, and the last remaining player wins.

Examples for D, L and M are:

'I love my love with a D, because his name is David, he is dashing, he comes from Denmark and I shall give him a Dalmatian.'

'I love my love with an L, because her name is Lydia, she is lovely, she comes from London and I shall give her a locket.'

'I love my love with an M, because his name is Mike, he is manly, he comes from Massachusetts and I shall give him a motorbike.'

... and I shall give him a dalmatian

Age range 6+
Number of players 2–4
Ideal for Keeping youngsters awake, alert
and happy on a daytime car journey
What you will need Refereeing skills, as
disputes will always arise as to who saw
which car first, or whether it is actually green
or more like blue

Colour collecting

This game will keep back-seat children entertained as they try to be the first to spot certain cars on the road.

How to play
Choose a colour. Players have to watch out for
cars of that colour and shout out when they see
one. A player scores a point each time he is the
first to see a car of the chosen colour, and the
first to 20 points is the winner.

It is best to choose a colour that is not too
common, or players will be shouting out all the
time and the game will end quite quickly. Thus
black and white are colours to be avoided.

Similarly, if you choose a rare colour such as
purple, the game might never end. Good choices
are colours like red or blue.

Variations
You could make the game more interesting
by having two colours, one, such as red,
which scores one point for the first to see it,
and another rarer one, such as orange or
yellow, which will score two points. Different
types of vehicle could also be incorporated,
so a lorry, bus and motorbike are all worth
extra points.

Overtaking
If you overtake a point-scoring car, and later
that same car overtakes you, the player who
spots it overtaking scores a point. This avoids
any arguments beginning 'You cannot have
that, we've seen it before'.

Quick on the draw

Age range 8+
Number of players 6+ (in teams)
Ideal for Family parties, since there is no upper age limit, and the only restriction on whether grandad plays is how fast he can run

This is a drawing and racing game which usually causes much amusement, particularly in the outlandish efforts of some players to draw fairly simple things.

Preparation

On about 20–30 slips of paper, write the names of a number of common objects – things that everybody will know, but that aren't necessarily easy to draw. The panel contains a suggested list. Fold the slips of paper and place them in a bowl on a table at one end of the room. Beside the bowl lay two piles of clean slips of paper and three pencils.

How to play

Choose two equal teams and sit them close to each other at the opposite end of the room to the table are placed the bowl and the slips of paper.

Each team nominates a player to be the first to take part. When the referee says 'Go', the two players cross to the table (they need not race). When both are there, each takes a blank slip of paper from one of the piles and a pencil. Then one of them takes a slip from the bowl, unfolds it and lays it on the table, so that each player can see what is written on the slip simultaneously.

The task of each player then is to draw as quickly (and as clearly) as possible the object written on the slip of paper. No words must be written on the drawing.

Each player rushes to be the first to hand the drawing to his team. He must then stand apart, and cannot give hints or encouragement to his team. The referee or referees must keep an eye open for cheating.

Any member of the team can call out what he or she thinks the object in the drawing is. The first to shout out what was originally written on the paper scores a point for the team. Any writing accompanying the drawing automatically gives the point to the other team. The referee's decision is final on all matters.

Once the drawing has been identified, the next two players, one from each team, go to the table and another slip is taken from the bowl. Play can continue until all members of both teams have had, say, two turns.

What you will need Several small squares
of paper (about 10 cm/4 in would do), two
pencils (plus a spare)

Suggested subjects
* A cucumber
* The pearly gates
* A black hole
* A magazine
* A dolphin
* An aspirin tablet
* A squirrel
* A fried egg on toast
* A toffee
* A mobile phone
* A shooting star
* A frog
* A bar of soap
* A lipstick
* A CD
* A rose
* Charlie Chaplin
* A jumbo jet
* A hippopotamus
* A hedgehog
* A wedding ring
* A big toe-nail
* A crocodile
* Three pairs of socks
* A push-chair
* A fire
* An alarm clock
* A walnut
* Two peas in a pod
* A parcel

Acrostics

Age range 10+
Number of players Any
Ideal for Family parties, as all ages can take part
What you will need Pencil and paper for each player

This is a game for anyone who can spell reasonably well, and has a wide vocabulary. Naturally, older players will be better than those of, say, ten years old, so in a gathering of mixed ages, perhaps teams of two or three could be formed, with the oldest helping the youngest.

How to play

A referee supplies all players, or teams, with small sheets of paper and a pencil. He then reads out a word of five letters or more. Each player writes the word down the left-hand side of the paper, and then writes the letters of the word in reverse order down the right-hand side of the paper. Each player or team then has three minutes to fill in the space between the pairs of letters with other letters to make new words.

When the referee calls time, everybody must put down their pencils, and all those who have completed proper words between each pair score a point for each word plus a bonus of ten points. Those who haven't completed all the words just score a point for each word.

The referee then reads out a second word and the players try again. After ten words, those players with most points win.

Examples

The effort for the word TWENTY scores 16 points. The lower effort for NUMBER scores five points:

Age range 10+
Number of players Any
Ideal for Family parties with older children
What you will need Pencil and paper for
each player

Categories

This quiet game will appeal to older children wishing to display their intelligence. Adults can play too, so this is a good game for parties where all ages are present.

Preparation
Draw up sheets of paper containing grids, as shown in the illustration. Across the top, write six subjects, as shown. The first column is left blank.

How to play
Each player is given a sheet of paper and a pencil. Players write their names on the top of their sheets, and then each player is asked to nominate a letter. The nominated letter is written down in the blank left-hand column of each player's sheet. Ask the players not to nominate X or Z, as these letters make the game difficult.

Players then have five minutes to fill in the other columns. They have to find a word beginning with each chosen letter for each of the six subjects, or categories, at the top of the sheet.

At the end of the five minutes, each player swaps his sheet with the player on his right, who checks it. The player with the most correct entries is the winner.

Other suggested categories, apart from those in the illustration, could be: colours, football teams, capital cities, parts of the body, rivers or fruits.

	Animal	Country	Flower	Footballer	Girl's name	Bird

Word couplings

Age range 10+
Number of players Any
Ideal for Parties where older children want to play word games with the adults
What you will need Pencil and paper for each player

This is a word game with a difference – players must think of pairs of words. It is a good game, as perfect scores of 26 are rare, and it will usually produce an outright winner.

How to play
Give each player a pencil and piece of paper. Ask the players to write the letters A to Z down the left-hand side of the paper. Choose and announce a letter, say P. Each player has to go through the alphabet writing down a two-word phrase for each letter, the second word of the phrase beginning with the letter P.

Several two-word couplings suggest themselves; for A, P; for instance, Apple Pie, Active Player, Auto Pilot, Arnold Palmer (proper names are allowed). The only restrictions are that the two words must make a recognizable pair, and that no word can be used twice in the list.

After a time limit, say ten minutes, the player with the highest number of phrases wins.

You can play the game as often as you like, but avoid letters like J, X or Z for the second word. As well as P, good letters are B, H, R, S and T.

A perfect score of 26, with P as the key letter, could be obtained as follows:

P	
A	pple Pie
B	iennial Plant
C	hristmas Present
D	ry Powder
E	aster Parade
F	ire Power
G	oose Pimple
H	arry Potter
I	deal Pair
J	unior Partner
K	ings Pawn
L	eading Part
M	obile Phone
N	ew Potato
O	pen Prison
P	retty Picture
Q	uiet Patch
R	ose Pink
S	and Pit
T	hird Place
U	gly Pig
V	ictoria Plum
W	indow Pane
X	mas Party
Y	oung Person
Z	oo Pass

Age range 10+
Number of players Any
Ideal for Parties where there are cerebral types wanting a testing game
What you will need Pencil and paper, a dictionary

Across and down

Those people who spend hours on newspaper crosswords may relish a game that gives the appearance of making up their own crosswords. But it can be very frustrating, especially when other players pick letters that are of no use to you at all.

How to play

Supply each player with a pencil and a sheet of paper. It is best if each piece of paper contains a grid like a crossword. For up to six players, a grid of six squares by six is a good size – for more than six players, perhaps seven by seven or eight by eight. A neat grid made in advance with a ruler and then photocopied is preferable to asking players to draw their own grids.

The first player calls out a letter of his choice which each player must enter in a square on their grids. The letter may be entered in any blank square, but it must be done immediately and it cannot be moved later to another square.

When all players have entered the letter on their grids, the next player calls out a letter, and this is entered likewise, and so on round the table or round the room.

The object is to enter the letters so that they make words, reading across or down. Words must consist of three letters or more. Proper nouns, abbreviations and foreign words do not count.

The game ends when the grids are completed, and each player passes his grid to the left for checking. Each word scores the number of letters it contains.

A letter can be used twice or more in different words; for instance, a line WANTON would score for WANTON (6), WANT (4), ANT (3) and TON (3). Not many lines like this will be achieved.

The winner is the player with the highest total. A dictionary is used to settle disputes over words.

S	L	A	N	T	M
I	C	E	U	O	A
F	H	A	T	E	D
T	I	R	E	D	L
T	I	M	E	V	E
P	L	A	Y	X	Y

Across:
Line 1 slant (5), ant (3)
Line 2 ice (3)
Line 3 hated (5), ate (3), hat (3)
Line 4 tired (5), red (3), ire (3)
Line 5 time (4), eve (3)
Line 6 play (4)

Down:
Line 1 sift (4),
Line 2 no points
Line 3 ear (3), arm (3)
Line 4 nut (3), tee (3),
Line 5 toed (4)
Line 6 mad (3), ley (3)

TOTAL: 70

One at a time

Age range 10+
Number of players Any
Ideal for Parties of all ages
What you will need Pencil and paper for each player

Players cannot be at a loss for words when playing this game. A whole string of words can follow on from the starting word, and the player with the longest string wins.

How to play

Pencil and paper are given to every player.

Each player is then asked to write the same word (chosen by the host) at the top of his sheet. Begin the game with a word of four letters, for example 'Care'.

The object is for each player to write beneath the word another four-letter word that differs in one letter only from the original word. The player continues to make a string of words, each different from the word above it by one letter only. A word can only be used once.

At the end of a given time, say five minutes, activity stops and the player with the longest string of words wins.

Follow this by giving all players a five-letter word, and after this game a six-letter word. Usually, the longer the initial word, the harder the game gets. In fact, choose your words in advance, and make sure they are alterable by one letter. A simple word like 'Please', for example, can hardly be developed at all.

Strings of four, five and six-letter words are shown.

CARE	RIVER	LETTER
CURE	RAVER	BETTER
CURT	RAVED	BUTTER
CART	RACED	BITTER
PART	PACED	LITTER
PERT	PARED	LATTER
PENT	CARED	LATHER
LENT	CARER	BATHER
LEND	CATER	RATHER
WEND	LATER	RASHER
WENT	MATER	DASHER
TENT	MATED	DASHED

Age range 10+
Number of players Any
Ideal for Family gatherings which include children aged 10 or more
What you will need Pencil and paper for each player

Guggenheim

This is a slightly more difficult version of Categories (see page 115).

Preparation

To make it easier and neater for the players, draw up in advance grids like the one in the diagram. The categories can either be chosen beforehand and written down the left-hand column, or the players can write them in on the day. There should be eight columns for the players to write in their choice of word for each category.

How to play

Each player has a pencil and paper. You then choose an eight-letter key word at random. A good way of doing this is to open a book at any page and pick the first eight-letter word to appear on the left-hand side. You read this word to the players and they write it across the top of the columns on their sheets, one letter above each column.

Each player now has ten minutes to write in each column opposite each category a word

Scoring

First of all, players score one point for each space filled in. Players then read out their words one at a time, column by column, and each player who has a word that nobody else has used scores an extra point for it.

corresponding to the category, which must begin with the letter at the top of the column. Because the letters are chosen at random, the grid is harder to complete than in the game Categories. There could be awkward letters, and some could be duplicated, which means that players might need to think of two instances of the category beginning with the same letter. If the eight-letter word was 'Dividend', as in the example, three of the columns will need filling with words beginning with D, and two with words beginning with I. Words cannot be repeated.

The blank sheet could look like that shown.

	D	I	V	I	D	E	N	D
Flower								
Town								
Food								
Boy's name								
Colour								
Tree								

Poetry please

Age range 10+
Number of players 8+ (in teams)
Ideal for Family parties with mixed age groups

This is a taxing but rewarding game which will test players' skills at writing poetry. It should be saved for a time when all remaining partygoers not in bed are at least ten years old, and it is suggested that it is played with teams of three or four players in a team so that the older and more poetic can combine with the younger and less eloquent.

Preparation

You should prepare a few groups of four words in advance. Each group of four will be used for one game. The words should be ordinary, straightforward words because they are to be fashioned into poems, which is hard enough as it is without trying to make words like 'expedient' or 'necessary' fit in. A suitable group of four might be: boy, duck, leg, day.

How to play

Divide the players into teams and issue each player with paper and pencil.

Explain the object of the game. You will read out four words. The teams have to write a poem of four lines, with one of the four words in each line.

The requirement of each poem is that the second and fourth lines rhyme. And one of the four words must be in the rhyme – it must be at the end of either the second or fourth line.

The teams have eight minutes to write their poems. You then ask each team in turn to read out their poem. You, as referee, will then be the judge as to which poem is the best. Tell them that humour is one objective and you will look kindly on poems that make you laugh.

This game, especially if any team can produce a funny poem, will bear repeating, so have a few groups of four words ready. You could include words that might lend themselves to funny verses, such as belly, feet and socks, but don't make things obvious by including, say, snickers.

What you will need Pencils and a supply
of paper

Suggested word and poem examples

Other suggestions for word groups:
Head, ears, belly, hat
Feet, socks, road, house
Night, wife, burglar, chips

Here are some efforts using the four groups
of words suggested above.

A boy with peculiar hobbies
Once hatched a duck from an egg
But one day he went and upset it
And suffered a bite on his leg

A man with a gigantic belly
And very protruding ears
Got a headache from watching the TV
Grabbed his hat and went out for some beers

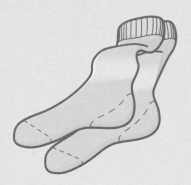

A man who lives down our road
Leaves the house to go shopping in frocks
He wears the latest high heels on his feet
But spoils it with holes in his socks

One night we were cooking our meal
When a burglar broke in, large as life,
He demolished my sausage and chips
And left after kissing the wife

What age and ate

Age range 10+
Number of players Any
Ideal for Family parties where all ages gather

This is another game for the older members of the party who have word skills. You will need to prepare beforehand.

Preparation
Make a list of about 12 to 20 words all with the same ending. This is not as difficult as it sounds as there are many words that end in '-age', '-ate', '-ation' and '-ment'.

Look them up in a dictionary, write a short definition of each word and add in brackets the word's initial letter. If you have a computer and printer you can type up a sheet like one of those displayed here and print off enough copies for all your competitors.

How to play
Issue a sheet and pencil to all players and give them a fixed time (say, ten minutes) to find and write down all the words that satisfy the definitions. At the end of the allotted time, players can swap papers and check each other's as you read out the answers. The player with most correct answers is the winner.

Team game
If you feel you have younger players who might not compete well, and/or players who are not as literate as others, you can ask them to form teams of, perhaps, three in a team, to level the chances.

What '-age' and '-ate'?

Definitions for words ending in '-age' (with initial letters)

1 To administer, to be in charge of (**M**)

2 To belittle, to speak contemptuously of (**D**)

3 Power rating of electricity (**W**)

4 To search for food (**F**)

5 The wine obtained from a harvest, usually referred to by year (**V**)

6 The residence of the local clergyman (**V**)

7 Union between man and woman (**M**)

8 Tea, coffee, beer and suchlike (**B**)

9 Where the car goes (**G**)

10 A religious journey (**P**)

11 To knead or rub parts of the body (**M**)

12 Typical or normal amount (a batsman has one) (**A**)

13 Cheapest accommodation on a ship (**S**)

14 A channel or corridor (**P**)

15 The bodice of a dress, or flowers pinned thereto (**C**)

What you will need Paper and pencil for each player

Definitions of words ending in '-ate'

1 To end (**T**)

2 To think deeply (**M**)

3 To lift, to move higher (**E**)

4 To show, or prove (or protest in a rally) (**D**)

5 Lying face-downwards (**P**)

6 Occurring after the scheduled time (**L**)

7 To divide or sort into parts (**S**)

8 One of those united in America (**S**)

9 To bring into existence (**C**)

10 To make something worse. Also to annoy (**A**)

11 To make easier to bear (like of pain) (**A**)

12 To make or pass laws (**L**)

13 A tile used in roofing (**S**)

14 A sum total of separate units (or football scores) (**A**)

15 A container, often containing bottles of beer (**C**)

Easy preparation

If you don't have a computer, you could issue the players with blank sheets of paper and read out the definitions, giving each player or team 30 seconds or so to write in the answers before moving on to the next one.

Answers

Ate: 1 Manage; 2 Disparage; 3 Wattage; 4 Footage; 5 Vintage; 6 Vicarage; 7 Marriage; 8 Beverage; 9 Garage; 10 Pilgrimage; 11 Massage; 12 Average; 13 Steerage; 14 Passage; 15 Corsage.

Ate: 1 Terminate; 2 Meditate; 3 Elevate; 4 Demonstrate; 5 Prostrate; 6 Late; 7 Separate; 8 State; 9 Create; 10 Aggravate; 11 Alleviate; 12 Legislate; 13 Slate; 14 Aggregate; 15 Crate.

Battleships

Age range 9+
Number of players 2+
Ideal for A quiet break in family parties, when all who wish can take part

This is a game usually played by two, but you could play with small teams of two or three players per team. If you have four teams, you can play two semi-finals followed by a final and a third-place game, so all are playing continuously.

Preparation

Rule up a number of grids (ten squares by ten squares is a good size), lettering the columns A to J at the top and rows 1 to 10 at the left.

How to play

Each player or team is given two grids and a pencil. Imagining the grid to be the sea, the player uses one grid to position his fleet. His fleet consists of one battleship (which occupies four adjacent squares, horizontal or vertical, on the grid), two cruisers (three squares), three destroyers (two squares) and four submarines (one square). These are indicated by lightly shading in the squares occupied. Vessels can only touch diagonally.

Each navy is also allowed to position four mines (one square each), marked by a circle, which can be deployed anywhere.

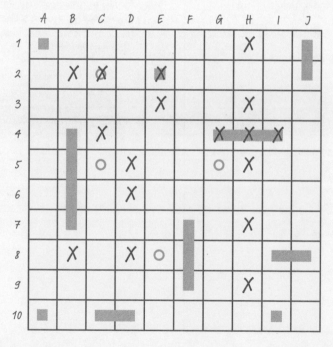

You have lost a cruiser and a submarine, but your opponent has hit one of your mines.

What you will need Sheets of paper containing ruled grids as illustrated, and a pencil for each player or team

Players toss to decide who goes first. The first player names a square, for example C3. His opponent puts a cross on C3 on his sheet. If there is a ship on that square, the opponent must acknowledge a hit, and state the class of ship hit. He then has a turn and the same process is followed.

Players name squares alternately in an effort to hit each other's ships. If a player hits a mine, he loses a turn. A submarine is sunk with one hit, but a battleship takes four hits.

The first player to sink all his opponent's ships is the winner.

Recording the shots

A player's shots are recorded on the second grid. When calling out a square, a player should record it with a tick if he registers a hit, and a cross for a miss. By this method he does not duplicate shots and he keeps a record of his opponent's ships that are sunk.

	A	B	C	D	E	F	G	H	I	J
1								X		
2		X	X		✓S					
3					X			X		
4			X				✓C	✓C	✓C	
5				X				X		
6				X						
7								X		
8		X		X						
9								X		
10										

If you have the chart opposite, your opponent will be recording his shots as on this grid.

Samuel Spade the gardener

Age range 8+
Number of players 3–10
Ideal for Parties where children are the same age, and of roughly the same capabilities, such as a group of school friends

This game is similar to the well-known card games called Go fish and Happy families, and is as simple. The fun comes from the outlandish names the children have to remember.

How to play

For up to six players: from the pack of cards take the Ace, King, Queen, Jack and 10 of each suit.

For seven or eight players: take the Ace, King, Queen, Jack, 10 and 9 of each suit.

For nine or ten players: take the Ace down to the 8 of each suit.

The dealer shuffles the cards and deals them out one at a time to the players, beginning with the player on his left, and including himself, until all the cards are gone. It does not matter if some players have one more card than others.

Each of these cards has a special name.

* The King of Spades is called Samuel Spade the gardener.
* The Queen of Spades is Samuel Spade the gardener's wife.
* The Jack of Spades is Samuel Spade the gardener's son.
* The Ace of Spades is Samuel Spade the gardener's servant.
* The 10 of Spades is Samuel Spade the gardener's dog.
* If used, the 9 of Spades is Samuel Spade the gardener's cat.
* If used, the 8 of Spades is Samuel Spade the gardener's canary.
* The King of Hearts is Henry Heart the butcher.
* The Queen of Hearts is Henry Heart the butcher's wife, the Jack is his son, the Ace is his servant, the 10 is his dog, the 9 his cat and the 8 his canary.
* The King of Diamonds is Dominic Diamond the jeweller, and as before the Queen is Dominic Diamond the jeweller's wife, the Jack his son, the Ace his servant, the 10 his dog, the 9 his cat and the 8 his canary.
* The King of Clubs is Clarence Club the policeman, and the Queen his wife, the Jack his son, the Ace his servant, the 10 his dog, the 9 his cat and 8 his canary.

What you will need A pack of playing cards

The object is to collect together all the cards of one family. When a player has obtained the whole of a family – for example, Dominic Diamond the Jeweller and his wife, son, servant and dog, and, if being used, his cat and canary – he lays them down on the table.

When the players have picked up their cards and looked at them, the player to the dealer's left starts the game by asking one of the other players for a card. For example, he might say: 'Hannah, have you got Clarence Club the policeman's dog?' If Hannah has this card she must hand it over, whereupon the asking player adds it to his hand. He then asks Hannah, or any other player, for any other card. So long as the player asked has the card, it must be handed over. The asking player keeps asking until the card he asked for is not held by the player he asked, when his turn ends; the turn to ask passes to the player on his left, and so on.

The asking player must ask for the card by its proper name. For example, he must ask for 'Clarence Club the policeman's dog' and not the 'Ten of Clubs'. If he gets the name wrong, his turn ends.

An asking player can ask for any card he likes, whether or not he has a card of the relevant suit in his hand. For example, he can ask a player for Samuel Spade the gardener's wife whether he has a Spade in his hand or not. It follows that when the second asking player's turn arrives, he can immediately ask for any cards the first asking player might have picked up on his turn. Of course, he's got to be able to remember them.

Family fortunes

In this game, fortunes may swing quickly, as a player with many cards in his hand can lose the lot at one turn. For example, the player whose turn it is when there are only two players left knows that all the cards not laid on the table and not in his hand are held by his opponent, who only has to ask for them one by one to acquire the lot, and at least one set. But of course he might make a mistake in asking for a card by its wrong name!

A player who runs out of cards, either because he has laid down a set or because he has had to give them to other players when asked, drops out of the game (but might still win if he has laid a set or two down).

The game ends when all cards have been laid down and the player with most sets is the winner.

Old maid

Age range 7–10
Number of players Any (4–8 is best)
Ideal for Amusing young children
What you will need For up to six players, one pack of cards; for more players, two packs of cards

Instead of a single winner, this game has a single loser, so avoid it if there are sensitive souls present.

Preparation
Remove from the pack (or two packs) one of the queens, so that an odd number of queens are left.

How to play
The cards are dealt until all are exhausted (it does not matter if some children have one more card than others).

The children look at their cards and lay down in front of them on the table any pairs (for example, two 3s, two kings) they hold. If a player holds three of a kind, he lays down a pair and keeps the third card.

The first player to go holds his remaining cards face-down and offers them to the player to his left. She takes one and adds it to her cards. If the card she receives makes a pair with a card in her

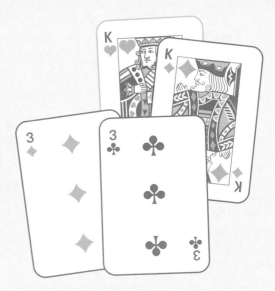

hand, she lays the pair down with the others.

Whether the accepted card makes a pair or not, she shuffles her cards and offers them in a fan face-down to the player on her left who takes one, and so on.

Players gradually drop out as the cards get discarded as pairs, and finally only the odd Queen is left. The player holding it is 'Old maid', and the loser.

Children are always anxious that a Queen in their hand gets passed on, and often show their pleasure when it is. As a result, the whereabouts of the odd Queen is often known, but this just seems to add to the excitement.

Age range 6–10
Number of players 2–6
Ideal for Entertaining children with a simple card game.
What you will need A pack of cards and the willingness to intervene if disappointed children don't play according to the rules

Fish

This is a very simple game, but also a simple one for young players to cheat, so keep a close watch.

How to play

One child is chosen as dealer, and deals five cards to each player including himself, the remainder being placed face-down in the centre of the table as the stock.

The object is to form sets of four cards of the same rank (for example, four 6s or four aces). The player on the dealer's left begins by naming another player and asking her to hand over all her cards of a certain rank ('Hannah, give me your 9s'). If Hannah has any 9s, she must hand them over. A player cannot ask for cards, however, without holding at least one card of the rank himself.

Should a player asked not hold a card of that rank, she says 'Fish', and the asking player takes a card from the stock. If the asking player successfully obtains a card he requests either from the player or the stock (in which case he shows it), he is entitled to another turn, and indeed keeps the turn until he is unsuccessful, when it passes to the player on his left.

As soon as a player obtains a set of four cards, he lays them down on the table in front of him. The winner is the player with most sets at the end, by which time all the cards will be on the table.

If, on his turn, a player has no cards, he takes one from stock, but must wait until his next turn before asking for a card from another player.

> **! WARNING**
> Young children who have collected three cards of the same rank have been known to throw tantrums when asked to hand them to a player holding the fourth one. You have been warned.

Beggar my neighbour

Age range 6–10
Number of players 2–8
Ideal for Introducing young people to card games
What you will need A pack of cards

This is often the first card game children learn. It requires no skill and children love winning a big pile of cards.

How to play

The dealer deals out all the cards face-down one at a time to all the players, including himself. It does not matter if some players get a card more than others. Players do not look at their cards, but square them up in a neat pile face-down in front of them.

The player to the dealer's left turns over her top card and lays it face-up in the centre. Each player in turn lays the top card of his pile face-up on top of it until an Ace, King, Queen or Jack appears.

If a player lays down an Ace, the following player must lay down, one at a time, four cards from his pile on top of it; if a King is laid down, the following player must lay three cards, if a Queen two cards and if a Jack one card. If, however, while doing this he himself lays down an Ace, King, Queen or Jack, he stops turning over his cards and the next player must add cards to the central pile in the same manner – four for an Ace, three for a King, and so on.

As soon as a player lays down the required number of cards without turning up an Ace, King, Queen or Jack, then the preceding player wins the whole pile. He turns the pile over and places it face-down below his existing face-down pile. He then turns over his top card and places it in the centre of the table to begin another round.

As players lose their cards, they drop out until only the winner is left, holding the complete pack.

Age range 6+
Number of players 2–8
Ideal for When a quiet spell would be
welcomed during a party; children will need
to concentrate very hard
What you will need A pack of cards

Pairs

**This game often goes under more fancy
names such as Pelmanism or
Concentration. It is a game of
concentration and memory, so there
could be significant differences in skill
level between children a year or two
apart in age. If some children struggle, it
might be best to change the game.**

How to play

The cards are laid out face-down in several rows
so a dining table or fairly large coffee table is
required. The cards should not be touching.

The first player to go (there is no real advantage
in going first) chooses two cards and turns them
over, showing them to the other players. If they
are a pair (for example, two 3s or two Jacks), he

keeps the pair and has another turn. If they are
not a pair, he puts them back face-down into the
places he took them from, and it is the turn of
the player to his left to try to pick a pair.

The object is to collect as many pairs as possible,
so each player must try to remember the cards
that have been looked at and returned by a
previous player.

After the first player, each player picks their cards
up one at a time so that if, for example, their first
card is a Queen, and a Queen has already been
exposed by a previous player, they can complete a
pair (provided they can remember where the
previous Queen was!).

When all the cards have been taken, the player
with the most pairs wins.

Donkey

Age range 7–10
Number of players 3–6
Ideal for Parties with young children
What you will need A pack of cards

This is a fast, somewhat silly game which keeps everybody alert throughout and usually causes laughter at the end.

Preparation

You do not need all the cards. You require one rank of four for each player. For example, if there are five players, you could use all the 2s, 3s, 4s, 5s and 6s. The rest are put to one side.

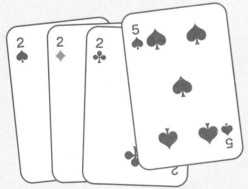

How to play

The cards are shuffled and the dealer deals them out one at a time face-down to all players, including himself. Everyone should have four cards.

Players look at their cards. The objective is to get a set of four cards of the same rank. The dealer calls 'Go' and all players select from their hands a card they don't want and put it down to their left. As soon as they've done this they can pick up the card to their right that their right-hand opponent has put down. They can then put down another card to their left and pick up another from their right and so on. No player can have more than four cards in his hand; in other words, he cannot pick up the card on his right until he has put down one on his left. It is in every player's interest to pass on as quickly as possible.

Soon, one player will complete a set of four of a kind. He lays his cards down quietly in front of him and places a finger against his nose. Other players will one by one spot this and also put down their cards and place a finger against their noses. The last to do so is the donkey, and loses.

Children will like to play this game again, so you could suggest playing until someone has been donkey three times, when he really is a donkey!

Age range 7–10
Number of players 2–12
Ideal for A party with children, but adults can play too
What you will need A pack of cards (or two packs if there are more than eight players)

Sevens

This is a game that goes under a variety of names, but children know the simplest version as Sevens.

How to play

A dealer is decided by any method. He deals all the cards out, one by one face-down beginning with the player to his left. Some players may get one card more than others, so if a few games are played the deal should circulate to the left.

The player to the dealer's left begins play by laying any 7 on the table. If she hasn't one, the next player to the left has the opportunity to lay one

and so on. Once a 7 is laid, then the 8 or the 6 of the same suit can be played to it. A 7 can always be played.

Once a suit is started, it gets built up in rows, from 7 up to King in one direction, and from 7 down to Ace in the other. Only one card is laid at a time. A player who cannot go must miss his turn.

A player must go if he can. He cannot hold back a card to stop the development of a suit. Of course, if he has a choice of cards to lay, he is entitled to choose the one that suits him best. The player who gets rid of all his cards first is the winner.

Rockaway

Age range 8–13
Number of players 2–8
Ideal for Parties with children over 8 years old

This is a simple game to understand which nevertheless occasionally gives the opportunity for skilful play. Players should hold on to Aces as long as they can and try to keep a good selection of suits and numbers in their hands to give them the maximum chance of being able to go when their turn comes round next.

How to play

The first dealer is chosen by any method – there is no advantage. After shuffling, the dealer deals seven cards face-down to each player, then turns the next card face-up in the centre of the table. This card is called the 'widow'. The rest of the cards are placed in a pile face-down beside it, and are called the stock.

Players take their cards into their hands, and the player to the dealer's left plays first. He must play a card to the widow, which can be one of three: a card of the same suit, a card of the same rank or an Ace.

If he has none of these, he must draw a card from the stock, and continue to do so until he draws a card that will go, which he plays. The following player must play a card to the new top card of the widow, and so on.

If the stock becomes exhausted, and a player cannot go, he merely 'knocks' and misses his turn. The hand ends when a player gets rid of all his cards, called 'going boom'. All other players then expose their hands and are debited on the score sheet with the total value of the cards they hold: aces count 15, court cards (King, Queen, Jack) count ten each, and the other cards have their pip value.

The deal passes round the table clockwise, and when everyone has dealt once, the winner is the player with the lowest debit score.

Variation

In Rockaway, the Ace is of special value in that it can always go. Thus players should keep hold of aces at least until an opponent is down to one card and therefore likely to go out next round, when it might be wise to ditch the Ace as it costs 15 points if caught in your hand. Some players give even more value to the Ace, in that a player who lays an Ace can change the suit to whatever he wants, e.g. if he lays the Ace of spades the suit doesn't automatically change to spades but to whatever suit the player specifies.

What you will need One pack of cards if there are up to five players, two packs for more than five, pencil and paper for scoring

Example hand

Players A, B, C, D hold the hands in the illustration. Player A dealt, and the widow is the ♥K. Player B is first to play and has to play ♥2. Player C plays ♥6 and Player D ♥J.

On the second round, Player A plays ♥3 (at this stage he holds back ♥A, even though it would cost 15 points if he were caught with it,

because an Ace can always go). Player B is now out of hearts but can play ♣3. Player C now has the choice of playing ♣K or ♦3. Although he would be pleased to get rid of his high-scoring ♣K, he would be advised to play ♦3, thus retaining at least one card of each suit in his hand. This guarantees that he will be able to go on the next round. And so on.

Ranter go round

Age range 8–12
Number of players Any
Ideal for Large parties of children, as up to 30 can play if necessary
What you will need A pack of cards, as many counters or coins to supply three for each player, a receptacle for the counters

This is a simple, fun game which could entertain as few as four or five children, a dozen sitting round a table, or even more sitting in a circle on the floor. Also called Cuckoo or Chase-the-Ace, it has been popular for at least three centuries and you can even buy specially made packs without suits with which to play the game.

How to play

All players are given three counters, one of which they will have to forfeit each time they lose a life, so if you are playing round a table, a bowl, saucer, or other receptacle should be placed in the centre of the table to receive the counters.

In this game the cards rank from King (high) down to Ace (low).

Any player may deal. The dealer shuffles the cards and gives one card face-down to each player, including herself. The object is to avoid being left holding the lowest card.

Each player looks at his card, and play begins with the player to dealer's left. He must decide whether to keep his card or swap it with the player on his left. Obviously, if he has a card that he considers is unlikely to be lowest, he will keep it. For example, if there are eight players and he holds a 10, he would think it extremely unlikely that all other players would hold a card of value 10 or above, so he wouldn't want to change it for what would in all probability be a lower card. However, if his card is a 3, he would change,

knowing that he could only lose if in the exchange he was given a 2.

To change, a player pushes his card towards his left-hand neighbour and says 'Change'. His neighbour must hand over his card, pick the one offered him and then has the option of changing with his left-hand neighbour, and so on.

The only occasion when a player may refuse to exchange cards is if he holds a King, which is the highest card. He merely says 'King' and exposes it face-up, forcing the player who wished to change to keep his card. The player to the left of the player with the exposed King then has the right to change or not with the player to his left.

If a player, in obeying a command to change, passes to his right an Ace, 2 or 3, he must announce this. This could tell succeeding players that their card is safe, so they would not demand a change.

The dealer is last to play, and if she wishes to change she must cut the remaining pack and change with the card at the top of the bottom half of the pack.

All players then expose their cards, the player or players holding the lowest card losing a life and putting a counter into the middle.

The deal passes to the left after each round. A player who loses his three counters drops out, and the last player remaining is the winner.

Age range 8–12
Number of players 4 or 6
Ideal for A small party where four or six children would like to play
What you will need A pack of cards, pencil and paper to score

Twenty-nine

This is a neat adding-up game, which requires little more skill than the ability to count to 29.

How to play

With four players, the full pack is used; with six players you remove any 10, 9, 8 and 2, thus reducing the pack to 48 cards.

In this game each card has a value. Picture cards count as one point only, as do the Aces, while all the other cards count as their pip value.

Any player may deal first (every player gets the chance to deal once during a game). The dealer shuffles the cards and deals them one at a time to each player, including himself, beginning with the player on his left. With four players, each player gets 13 cards, with six each player gets eight cards.

The player to dealer's left chooses a card and plays it face up to the centre of the table. She announces its value. The next player to the left places a card face up on top and announces the

Variation
The game can be played with five players by removing a 10 and 9 from the pack, reducing it to 50 cards, or 10 per player. The game is played in the standard way, but the last pile will add up only to 10, and not 29. The last player to put a card on it wins it.

value of the two cards added up. For example, if the first player lays a 10, and calls 10, the second player might decide to lay, say an 8, in which case he would call 18. Players continue to add cards to the pile in turn clockwise round the table.

The object for each player is to try to make the total 29. If a player can make the total 29, he wins all the cards in the pile and puts them face down in front of him. The player to his left begins a new pile.

The suits of the cards are immaterial. The total of the pile can never rise above 29, and a player must always go if he can. For example, if the total reaches 26, the next player can win the pile by laying a 3. If he hasn't a 3, but has a 1 or 2 he must lay it. If he has only cards of value more than 3, he cannot go. Once a player has played all his cards, he takes no further part in that deal.

Once all the cards have been played, each player scores a point for each card he has won. The score is entered on the sheet, and when each player has dealt once, the scores are added up and the player with the highest total wins.

Cheat!

Age range 8–12
Number of players 3–12
Ideal for Amusing children with a noisy card game

This is a popular game in which sometimes, in fact often, you have to lie or cheat. Children love shouting out 'Cheat!' to each other, even though it might cost them a chance of winning if they're wrong.

How to play
Each player draws a card from the pack, and the player with the highest card (Ace is high) deals.

The whole pack (or double pack) is dealt out one at a time face-down beginning with the player on the dealer's left. The object of the game is to get rid of all your cards.

The player on the dealer's left begins play by placing a card to the centre of the table face-down, at the same time announcing its rank (for example, 2, 6 or King). She may announce the true rank or she can lie and pretend it is any other card.

Suppose the player lays down a card and announces 'Queen'. The next player must lay a card face-down on top of it and announce the next highest rank upwards, in this case 'King'. That player may have a King, and can lay it. But if she hasn't got a King, she must choose any other card she holds and lay it announcing 'King'. So here she is cheating. The next player must lay a card and announce 'Ace', but of course only she knows if it really is an Ace.

In this game, Ace ranks both high and low, so the sequence runs Queen, King, Ace, 2, 3 and so on – in other words it is a never-ending sequence.

Each player on his or her turn must lay a card and must announce the requisite rank, whether the card is that rank or not.

The laying of cards continues until a player challenges another with the cry of 'Cheat!'. The player who is challenged must then turn over the card she has just laid. If she has been caught out cheating, and the card is not of the rank she said it was, she must take all the cards on the table into her hand, plus any two cards that the successful accuser wants to give her from his own hand. However, a player cannot hand over these two bonus cards if they are the only cards she holds – she must retain at least one card in her hand. Getting rid of these two cards is a bonus for the successful accuser, and it is to encourage players to cry 'Cheat! – it is tempting for some ultra-cautious players to leave all the challenging to others.

If the player who is challenged has not been cheating, and the card is as she said, then the challenger takes all the cards into his hand.

If two or more players call 'Cheat!' simul-taneously, then the player nearest to the left of the player challenged is the one deemed to have made the challenge.

The player forced to take the cards into her hand begins the new round of play by laying any card

What you will need A pack of cards – if
more than eight players, two packs

from her hand and announcing its rank (truly or
falsely, as she wishes, of course).

The first player to get rid of their cards wins. Of
course, as soon as a player lays her last card
somebody should cry 'Cheat!'. It is probable she
is cheating, so instead of winning she will have to

pick up the pile from the table. The game can thus
go on for a long time before somebody actually
does win.

Children love this game and will probably demand
countless repeats.

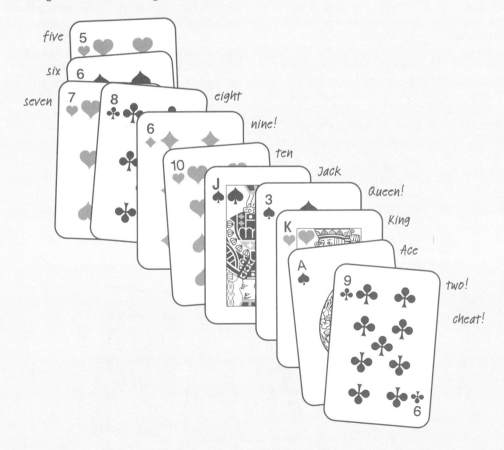

My ship sails

Age range 8–12
Number of players 3–7
Ideal for Amusing up to seven children
What you will need A pack of cards

This game is similar to Donkey (see page 132), and will please children as they try to collect a set of seven cards of the same suit.

How to play

Anyone can deal (there is no advantage), and the dealer deals seven cards face-down to each player.

Each player's object is to collect seven cards of the same suit. So when players pick up their cards and examine them, they will decide (without telling the other players, of course) which suit (hearts, clubs, diamonds or spades) they will collect. It will be the suit they have most cards of to start with.

Once players have looked at their hands, they all place a card face-down to their left. When

everyone has done this, the dealer calls 'Go' and each player picks up the card to his right which his neighbour has placed there, adding it to his hand.

This continues for round after round, with players retaining cards of the suit they are collecting, and passing on to their left-hand neighbour cards of the other suits.

Eventually one player will have a hand of seven cards all of the same suit. Instantly he calls out 'my ship sails', and lays the seven cards out in a line.

It is possible that two or more players complete a winning hand on the same round, in which case the player who calls 'My Ship Sails' first is the declared winner.

Sometimes, of course, two players will, without knowing it, be collecting the same suit, which will make it harder for them to win. If there are more than four players, this is a certainty as there are only four suits.

Rolling stone

Age range 8–12
Number of players 4–6
Ideal for Amusing a small group of children
What you will need A pack of cards

This is an intriguing game which contains an element of trick-taking.

Preparation

You will need to reduce the pack according to the number of players. For six players, remove the 2s, making a 48-card pack. For five players, remove the 2s, 3s and 4s, making a 40-card pack. For four players, remove the 2s, 3s, 4s, 5s and 6s, making a 32-card pack.

How to play

Each player takes a card from the pack, the player with the highest (Ace high) becoming dealer. He deals out the pack one at a time face-down to all the players, who should each receive eight cards.

The object is to be the first to get rid of all your cards.

Players look at their hands, and the person to the dealer's left lays a card face-up on the table. Each player in turn to the left must lay a card of the same suit on top of it.

If all players are able to do this, the player who laid the highest card (Ace high) wins all the cards, which are called a 'trick'.

He lays the cards to one side, and they take no further part. He then lays down a card face-up from his hand to begin the next trick.

If a player doesn't have a card of the suit laid on the table, he must on his turn pick up all the cards on the table and place them in his hand. He then lays down a card of another suit to begin the

next trick (he is not allowed to lay down a card of the suit he has just picked up).

The tricks won are of no value – the winner is the first player to get rid of all his cards. It is an amusing game because time and again a player will get his hand down to one card and then be forced to pick up others.

Dingo

Age range 10+
Number of players Any
Ideal for Entertaining children while
sharpening up their arithmetic

This game is played like **Bingo**. It is Bingo
with dice, hence its name Dingo. It is
suggested that players cross out the
numbers on their cards as they achieve
them, otherwise you would need to
supply up to 15 counters or buttons for
each player.

Preparation

You will need to make the cards, as illustrated. Six
versions are suggested, the numbers being
arranged on each to give them all similar chances
of winning. Notice five numbers (17, 19, 27, 28,
29) are missing because in this game they are
impossible to get. It doesn't matter, incidentally, if
all players had the same cards because each
player makes their own individual numbers with
the dice. If you have a computer and printer, you
could make and print a number of differing cards.

How to play

Each player is given a Dingo card, and each rolls
the two dice to determine who goes first, the
highest scorer having that honour.

The first player throws the two dice, and she can
choose one of four different ways to use the two
numbers thrown to cross off a number or
numbers on her card. Suppose she throws a
2 and a 6, she can:

1 Use the two numbers separately to cross off
2 and 6
2 Add them together, to cross off 8
3 Multiply them, to cross off 12
4 Join them as a two-digit number, to cross
off 26

She can use her numbers in any of the four
options, but one only. For instance, with 2 and 6
she cannot cross off both 8 and 26. She must
choose. Usually it will pay to cross off the
numbers over 12 first, if the opportunity occurs,
as they are more difficult to achieve. The hardest
numbers on the cards are 22 and 33, which can
be obtained by only one throw (2, 2 and 3, 3).

Occasionally a player may find that she cannot
use one or even both of her numbers, in which
case she forfeits them. A player who throws a
double can use the numbers as she wishes, and
have another throw.

When a player has crossed off her number or
numbers, she passes the dice and pencil to the
player on her left, who has their turn, and so on.
The first to cross off all their numbers wins.

What you will need Two dice, a shaker, a number of home-made Dingo cards, a pencil

1	2				6
	8	9		11	
		15	16		
	20		22	23	
	26				30
		33		35	

	2	3		5	
7		9			12
	14	15	16		
		21	22	23	
	26				
				35	36

		3	4	5	
7			10	11	
	14	15	16		
			22		24
25					
31	32				36

1	2				6
	8	9			12
13	14				18
		21			24
	26				30
	32				36

1			4		6
	8		10		
		15	16		18
	20	21			24
25					
31			34	35	

	2	3	4		
		9	10	11	12
		15			18
		21			24
25					
		33	34	35	

Age range 7–10
Number of players Any
Ideal for A party where a group of young people want to do something on their own for a while
What you will need Two dice (plus pencil and paper for scoring if the players insist, but it is more fun without)

Fifty

This is the simplest of all dice games, in that children can sit on the floor and play it with only two dice, keeping running totals of their scores in their heads.

How to play

The players sit, either on the carpet or round a table. To decide who goes first, they all roll the dice and the highest total goes first. If two or more tie for highest, they have a repeat throw among themselves to see who goes first.

When the first thrower has been decided, he throws the dice, and thereafter the turn to throw goes round to the left.

The only scoring comes from throwing doubles:

Double-six	scores 25 points
Double-five	
Double-four	All these score 5
Double-two	points
Double-one	
Double-three	Loses all the score you have made so far

Before a player throws, he announces his score so far, and when he has made his throw, he announces his new score, passing the dice to the next player.

The winner is the first player to reach 50.

Each player's score rises gradually by steps of five, with the big moments coming with the throw of a double-six (25 points) or a double-three, when everybody laughs at the unfortunate player whose score reverts to nothing.

Age range 8+
Number of players Any
Ideal for Those periods during a family
party when a simple yet exciting game
is required
What you will need One die, a pencil and
a sheet of paper

Pig

**In this game, players can decide for
themselves when their turn ends. It is a
question of being happy with what you've
got or trying for a bit more at the risk of
losing all.**

How to play

All the players sit round a table and throw the
single die in turn. The player throwing the lowest
number goes first. If two or more tie, they throw
again until the tie is broken.

The first player throws the die and announces the
score. He can throw it again as often as he likes,
keeping a running score by adding the result of
each throw to his previous total. However, if he
throws a 1, his turn ends, and he loses all his
score for that turn.

Unless he throws a 1, therefore, a player must
decide when he wants to stop. When he stops, his
score is written down and the die passes to the
player on his left.

The die is passed round with each player either
recording a score or throwing a 1. The scores for
each round are added up as play progresses and
the first player to reach 101 wins.

On average, a 1 will be thrown every six throws,
and a player whose score on one turn gets into
the 20s might consider that a reasonable score to
stop at.

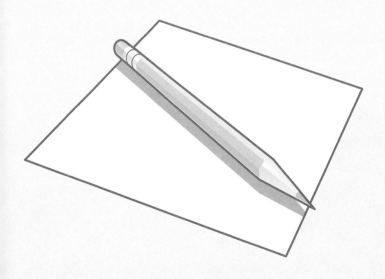

Beetle

Age range 8+
Number of players 2–8
Ideal for Parties with children who like drawing
What you will need A die, plus pencil and paper for each player

This is a race to draw a beetle (see illustration). Any more than eight players could make the game a bit tedious.

How to play

Each player throws the die to see who goes first, the highest scorer getting the privilege. The turn then passes from player to player to the left, and each player on her turn throws the die once.

As soon as a player scores a 1, she may begin to draw her beetle. A 1 stands for the body, and the body is always the first thing to be drawn. Once started, a player on each turn can add one item to the drawing provided she throws the right number. When the body is drawn, a 3 will add all three legs to one side of the body, a 6 will add the tail and a 2 the head. Once the head is attached to the body (but not before), each 4 thrown will add an eye, and each 5 thrown will add a feeler.

To draw the complete beetle, therefore, takes a 1, a 2, two 3s, two 4s, two 5s and a 6. But remember, the body has to come first, and the head has to be attached before the eyes and feelers can be added, so there will be wasted throws and it could easily take 20 or more throws to complete the drawing. The first to do so, of course, wins.

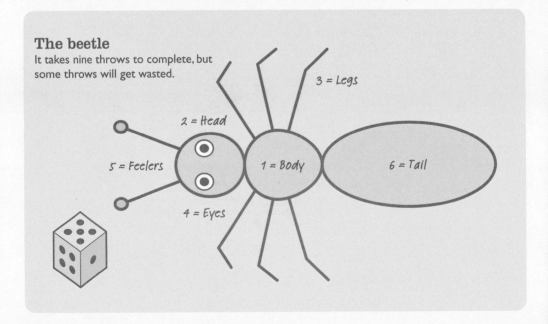

The beetle
It takes nine throws to complete, but some throws will get wasted.

3 = Legs
2 = Head
5 = Feelers
1 = Body
6 = Tail
4 = Eyes

Age range 8–12
Number of players 2–8
Ideal for A children's party (it encourages a little simple arithmetic)
What you will need Two dice, a drawing of a clock face (see illustration), a pencil for each player

The clock face

In this game, the players throw the dice in turns and race to cross off all the numbers on a clock face. Each player's clock face must be kept in full view so that all players can see which number is being tried for with each throw.

Preparation
If you have a computer and a printer, you could make a clock face and print off a copy for each player.

How to play
Players throw the two dice to determine who goes first (highest first). The turn thereafter passes to the left.

Players in turn throw the two dice and cross off the numbers 1 to 12 on the clock face as they score them, but they must be scored in the correct order from 1 o'clock to 12 o'clock.

For the numbers 1–6
A player can get the number with one die, or by adding the two together. For example, if she is on 4 o'clock, she can get her four by throwing 4 with one of her dice, or by throwing 1, 3 or 2, 2. When on 1 to 6, she can also cross out two numbers at once if they are in sequence. For example, if she needs 2 for 2 o'clock, and she throws 2, 3, she can cross out both 2 o'clock and 3 o'clock.

For the numbers 7–12
A player can get these only by adding the numbers on her two dice. However, there are often two or three ways to get these numbers; for example, 7 can be obtained with a 6, 1 or 5, 2 or 4, 3.

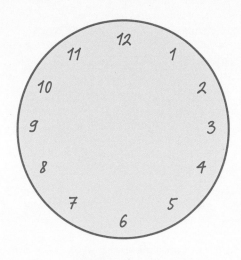

Variation
For a quicker game, you could allow players to cross off the numbers in any order. This means they can start crossing out from the first throw.

Drop dead

Age range 8+
Number of players 2–8
Ideal for A quiet period in a party when you can get the children seated round a table

This game provides the pleasure of throwing five dice, with each player's turn continuing for seven or eight throws while he or she racks up a good score.

How to play
Write the players' names on the score-sheet and record their scores for each round.

The first player throws the five dice (there's no advantage to throwing first or last). He scores the total of all the dots showing unless he throws a 2 or a 5 among the five dice. If any die or dice shows 2 or 5, he scores nothing for that particular throw and furthermore he removes any die showing 2 or 5. He can, however, continue his turn by throwing the remaining dice and scoring the total of the dots, again unless a 2 and/or a 5 are included in his throw.

A player's turn continues with him throwing the dice and adding his scores together as he goes, but every time he throws a 2 or 5, that die is removed. Eventually he runs out of dice altogether and his turn ends – he is said to have 'dropped dead'. His total is then entered on the score-sheet, and he hands the five dice to the player on his left.

Play ends when all the players have had five turns. Their scores are then totalled on the score-sheet, and the player with the highest total wins.

How a player's turn might develop is shown in the example. He drops dead at 35, which represents a fairly average score.

Example
The player avoids a 2 or a 5 on his first throw, but loses dice on his second, fourth, fifth and eighth throws.

Throw 1
Score: 17 Running score: 17

Throw 2
Score: 0 Running score: 17

Throw 3
Score: 9 Running score: 26

Throw 4
Score: 0 Running score: 26

Throw 5
Score: 0 Running score: 26

Throw 6
Score: 6 Running score: 32

Throw 7
Score: 3 Running Score: 35

Throw 8
Score: 0 Running score 35

What you will need Five dice, a plastic
cup, pencil and paper for scoring

Throw 1	1	6	3	3	4
Throw 2	4	3	1	6	4
Throw 3	4		1	3	1
Throw 4	2		1	6	3
Throw 5			5	2	1
Throw 6					6
Throw 7					3
Throw 8					5

Chicago

Age range 8+
Number of players Any
Ideal for Family parties where a game for all ages is required

In this game, players try to throw all the numbers it is possible to throw with two dice. They have two attempts to roll each number, using two dice each time. The lead can change frequently as the high-scoring numbers come at the end.

Preparation

Draw up a score-sheet with all the players' names written across the top and the numbers 2 to 12 down the left-hand side. Add a line for totals at the bottom (see illustration).

How to play

There is no need to throw dice to see who goes first, as there is no advantage, and indeed on each throw a different player could start.

In the first round, all the players try to throw the lowest total possible with two dice, which is 2 (two 1s). Each player has two attempts, and a player who succeeds scores five points for succeeding plus two points as a bonus (two being the number attempted).

In the second round, each player has two attempts at the number 3 (achieved by throwing a 2 and a 1). Success brings five points plus three. And so on to the last round, where success brings 17 points (five plus the bonus of 12). At the end, each player's scores are totalled, and the player with most points wins.

Opposite is a possible outcome of a game between four players – Lydia, Jonny, Isobel and Oliver – with the relevant scorecard shown.

Combinations

There are 36 ways in which two dice may fall, with 7 the likeliest number to result. The 36 ways result in these totals:

What you will need Two dice, a pencil, a score-sheet

throw	Lydia	Jonny	Isobel	Oliver
2				
3				
4				
5				
6				
7				
8				
9				
10				
11				
12				
Total	43	49	33	25

Golf

Age range 10+
Number of players 2–6
Ideal for Parties that might include a golf fan or two who'd like a game that slightly simulates its scoring

This is a game where you play six 'holes' and try to play them in as few 'strokes' as possible. You end up with something that vaguely resembles a golf score.

Preparation

Draw up an overall score-sheet on which the players' names are listed down the left-hand side. The diagram shows a score-sheet for five players. The numbers relate to the numbers of the 'holes'.

How to play

It doesn't matter in which order you play, but you can each roll the dice, the highest aggregate scorer going first, the second highest going second and so on.

The first player rolls the dice and, according to how they fall, decides which hole he is going to play first. It will normally be the hole corresponding to any doubles or trebles he achieves in the throw. For example, if he throws 1, 2, 5, 5, 6, he will choose to play hole 5, since to complete hole 5 he has to have all five dice showing 5 uppermost.

If a player had the throw 1, 2, 5, 5, 6, he would set aside the two 5s and throw the other dice again. Any 5s he threw would be added to the first two, and he would then re-throw the dice. He would continue to throw all the dice not showing 5 until finally all showed 5. The number of throws he took would be the number to be recorded for that hole.

The dice are passed round and when all players have completed a hole, the first player tackles a second hole, and so on until all players have completed six holes. Each player's scores are then added together to represent their scores for the 'round'.

Of course, a player's option to choose the hole he wishes to play based on his first throw becomes less valuable as the game progresses. A player with only holes 2 and 4 to play, for example, might throw 1, 3, 3, 5, 6 with his first throw. He must still choose which of holes 2 and 4 to play and throw all the dice again having used one throw without achieving anything. Scores will thus tend to be bigger for the last hole played than for the first.

What you will need Five dice, a plastic
cup, pencil and paper for scoring

	1	2	3	4	5	6	Total
Jack							
Sophie							
Ian							
Lucy							
Martin							

Yacht

Age range 10+
Number of players 2+ (up to 6 is best)
Ideal for A small party looking for a dice game that requires thought as well as luck

This is one of the best dice games, and can be enjoyed by players of all ages. Throughout the game, players have to make choices – do they risk all on going for a high-scoring combination, or do they settle for a safe but comparatively small score?

Preparation

Prepare in advance a score-sheet as shown; if you have a computer and printer, make half-a-dozen.

How to play

Write each player's name at the top of one of the columns on the score-sheet. Each player then throws the five dice in turn to determine who goes first – the player with the highest total throws first. The turn to throw passes to the left.

The object is to throw as many as possible of the patterns shown on the score-sheet. The panel describes the patterns and the scoring systems.

On her turn, a player throws the five dice, and then nominates one of the patterns to attempt.

The Patterns

Ones Only the 1s thrown score – two 1s scores two points

Twos Only the 2s score – two points each

Threes Only the 3s score – three points each

Fours Only the 4s score – four points each

Fives Only the 5s score – five points each

Sixes Only the 6s score – six points each

Little straight 1, 2, 3, 4, 5 – scores 30 points

Big straight 2, 3, 4, 5, 6 – scores 30 points

Full house Three of one number and two of another – for example 3, 3, 3, 5, 5 – scores total pip value plus 10.

Four of a kind Four of any one number scores total pip value of the four, plus 10.

Choice An attempt to score as many as possible, irrespective of the pattern. The score is total pip value, so 6, 6, 5, 5, 3 scores 25 points.

Yacht All five dice showing the same number scores 50 points irrespective of the number.

A player who nominates little straight, big straight, full house, four of a kind or yacht and fails to make it scores no points for that throw.

What you will need Five dice, a plastic cup, a prepared score-sheet and pencil

	Alan	Jane	Rose	Chas	John	Sarah
Ones						
Twos						
Threes						
Fours						
Fives						
Sixes						
Little straight						
Big straight						
Full house						
Four of a kind						
Choice						
Yacht						
TOTAL						

She must announce it so that all can hear. She then has two more throws in which she can re-throw as many of the dice as she wishes.

For example, if a player throws 5, 5, 2, 2, 1, she might nominate any of the following:

Fives She re-throws 2, 2, 1. She has a guaranteed ten points.

Four of a kind She re-throws 2, 2, 1 and if in her two re-throws she gets two more 5s, she scores 30 points – if she fails she scores nothing.

Full house She re-throws just the 1, hoping that in her re-throws she might get a 5 (score 29) or a 2 (score 26).

Yacht She re-throws 2, 2, 1 hoping to get all 5s for a score of 50.

Little straight She re-throws 5, 2, hoping to get 3, 4, giving her 30 points.

Choice She re-throws 2, 2, 1, hoping for a high pip total.

A player can only score by getting the pattern she nominated – if she gets another pattern she cannot score (except if she goes for four of a kind and gets yacht, where she scores for her four of a kind). A player can nominate a pattern only once. Her score is entered on the score-sheet after each turn, even if it is 0, so that at the end of the game each player will have had 12 throws. The player with the highest total wins.

Squares

Age range 9+
Number of players 2–8
Ideal for An undemanding dice game for a quieter period of a party

This is an attractive, simple game which can be amusing and frustrating at the same time. As the board gets filled up, opportunities to get rid of one's counters become fewer and the game can take a long time. But everybody is in with a chance right to the end.

Preparation

On a piece of cardboard of about 30 cm (12 in) square, draw up a grid of 36 squares, numbered as shown. Make a set of eight counters for each player by cutting squares or circles of card of a size that will fit into the squares on your grid. Each player's set of counters should be of the same colour, and different from everybody else's. If you use white card, you could leave one set of eight white and, with paints or coloured pencils, make sets of black, red, blue, green, yellow and so on.

How to play

The board is set in the centre of the table, with the players seated around. Each player throws the dice to determine who throws first (it is an advantage). The player with the highest score has the first turn and thereafter the turn passes to the left around the table.

The object of each player is to get rid of his counters as quickly as possible by placing them on the board.

Each player on his turn throws the two dice and places a counter onto a blank square on the board according to the number thrown. The numbers on the two dice can be used in three ways: they can be added, subtracted or used as separate digits to make a two-digit number. Thus, a throw of 2, 5 could be used to cover the squares 3 (5–2), 7 (5+2) or 25. Both numbers thrown on the dice must be used in this way, and a number cannot be used singly. For instance, a player throwing 5, 2 could not use the numbers separately to cover both squares 2 and 5, nor could he use one number only and discard another (so that he could not cover the 2 and ignore the die showing 5).

There are special rules for a throw that produces a double. Any double except double-1 allows a player to put a counter on any number on the board he wishes. This is useful, since eight numbers (17, 18, 19, 20, 27, 28, 29, 30) can be covered only by throwing a double. A double-1, however, incurs a penalty. The player to the right of the thrower is allowed to remove one of the thrower's counters from the board and return it to the thrower's pile.

Each player is allowed one throw of the dice on each turn. If the throw cannot be used – for example, if it is 4, 5 and both squares 1 and 9 are occupied – then the turn passes without the thrower being able to place a counter on the board.

The winner is the first player to place all his counters on the board. If there are six or more players, it is possible for the board to be full before any player has got rid of all his counters, in which case the player with fewest counters left wins.

What you will need Two dice, a home-
made board, a set of eight counters for each
player (see page 156)

1	2	3	4	5	6
7	8	9	10	11	12
13	14	15	16	17	18
19	20	21	22	23	24
25	26	27	28	29	30
31	32	33	34	35	36

Block game

Age range 8+
Number of players 2–6
Ideal for A small party where perhaps a few people would like a quiet game

The Block game is the basic game of dominoes, and there are several ways of playing it, some being more popular in particular countries than others. A simple game for four players is described first, with variations given later.

How to play

The full set of 28 dominoes is spread face-down on the table and shuffled around. Players take seven dominoes each and look at them. The usual way to see your dominoes during the game is to stand them on one of their long edges with the spots facing you, in such a manner that you can see your hand but the others players cannot. The object is to get rid of all your dominoes.

The player holding the double-6 goes first by laying it in the centre of the table. The turn now moves to the left, with the next player being required to lay a domino of which one side is a 6 against the starter domino. If the domino played is the 6–4, then the next player must lay a domino that matches either the 6 or 4. This is laid against the 6 or 4 already on the table. Thus a chain is formed, and each player on his turn can play a domino to either end of it. If he hasn't a domino that will go, he passes.

It is customary when playing a double to the table to place it a right angles to the chain, as the illustration of the beginning of a game shows. Corners can be turned when necessary in a similar way.

The first player to get rid of all his dominoes wins that round and the other players are debited with the total number of spots on the unplayed dominoes in their hands. The scores are recorded and it is customary to play five games, after which each player's scores are added up and the player with the lowest total is the winner.

For two or three players

If there are two or three players, it is customary to leave the undealt dominoes face-down in a 'bone yard' (so-called because originally dominoes were made of bone). A player who cannot go must take a domino from the bone yard. He can play this to the centre if it goes. If not, he adds it to his hand and passes. The last two bones in the bone yard must not be taken. When the bone yard is exhausted (so there are only two bones left), the player merely passes. If no player holds the double-6, the highest double held goes first.

For five or six players

If there are five or six players, each player begins with four dominoes, there being eight and four dominoes left in the bone yard respectively.

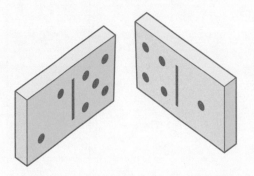

What you will need A standard set of
dominoes, pencil and paper to score

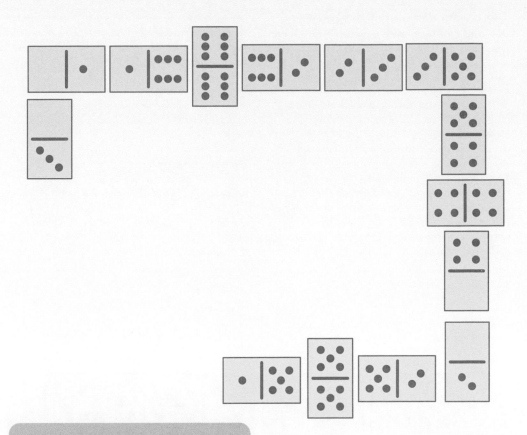

Sebastopol
In this variation, when a double is played it is
laid across the chain, and each end is available
to be played on – a new chain is begun at
right angles to the previous one.

Blind Hughie

Age range 8+
Number of players 2–5
Ideal for Introducing young children to dominoes
What you will need A standard set of dominoes

This is a domino game that requires no skill and can be played by young children (perhaps with adult supervision).

How to play

To choose a dealer, the dominoes are shuffled face-down and each player turns one over. The player with the highest double is the dealer; if no doubles are turned, the highest total spots deals.

The dominoes are turned over again and reshuffled. The dealer gives dominoes face-down to all players including herself: if two or three players, seven dominoes each; if four or five players, five dominoes each. The dominoes not dealt are put aside and not used.

The players do not look at the faces of their dominoes, but lay them in a neat row face-down in front of them.

The player on the dealer's left turns over her left-hand domino and places it in the centre of the table. The next player on her left then turns over her left-hand domino. If one end matches one of the ends of the domino on the table, then she places the matching ends together to begin a chain. If her domino will not go, she turns it over again and places it face-down at the right-hand of her row.

The next player then turns over her left-hand domino and plays it to the table or not in the same manner, and so on round the table.

The first player to get rid of all her dominoes wins. If the game gets blocked and nobody can go, there is a redeal.

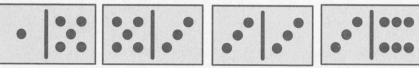

Age range 8+
Number of players 4
Ideal for When specifically four people would like a domino game
What you will need A standard set of dominoes

Ends

This is a game where a little skill can be exercised. It is different to most domino games in that dominoes are passed from one player to another.

How to play
The dominoes are placed face-down on the table and shuffled. Each player takes seven.

Players arrange their dominoes so that they can see them and the player with the double-6 plays it to the table.

Players in turn to the left then play a domino to the table so that one end matches one of the ends of the chain, as in the Block game (see page 158).

If a player cannot go, she asks the player on her left for a domino that will go. If she gets one, she plays it to the table and the player on her left then has her turn. This is where the player asked for a domino can show some skill. If she has two that will go, she hands over one that will enable herself to go on her turn.

If the player asked for a domino does not have one that will go, she must ask the player on her left, and so on. When a suitable domino is passed

over, it is passed back round the table to the original player who asked, and she plays it. Play then proceeds as usual.

If the question goes all round the table with nobody being able to supply a suitable domino, the original asker can play whichever domino she likes, and play again proceeds.

The winner is the first player to get rid of all her dominoes.

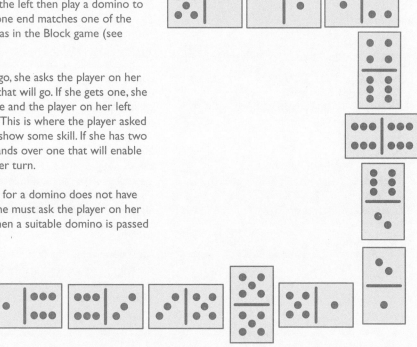

Fives and threes

Age range 8+
Number of players 2–5
Ideal for Up to five players who want a more advanced domino game

This is a dominoes game where the best players are good at arithmetic, since the object is to make the totals at each end of the domino chain add up to a number that divides by five or three. Children quick at sums should shine.

How to play
The first player is chosen by spreading the dominoes face-down on the table and each player picking one. Highest double goes first – if nobody has a double, all pick a second domino and so on. The dominoes are then returned face-down and the whole lot shuffled.

Scoring multiples
3	scores 1	(for one 3)
5	scores 1	(for one 5)
6	scores 2	(for two 3s)
9	scores 3	(for three 3s)
10	scores 2	(for two 5s)
12	scores 4	(for four 3s)
15	scores 8	(for five 3s and three 5s)
18	scores 6	(for six 3s)
20	scores 4	(for four 5s)

If two or three are playing, each player takes seven dominoes; if four play, each takes six; and if five play, each takes five. Remaining dominoes are placed to one side and take no part in the game.

The first player lays any domino to the table; the next player on the left can then lay a domino against it providing one end matches one end of the domino on the table, as in the Block Game (see page 158). A player must go if he can.

The object of the game is to score points by laying a domino such that the total of spots at each end of the chain is a multiple of either five or three.

If the total is nine, it scores 3 points (three 3s), if it is ten, it scores 2 points (two 5s) and so on. Doubles are laid across the chain and both ends count, enabling higher scores. For example, double-6, double-3 makes 18 (for six points), while double-6, double-4 makes 20 (for four points). The panel shows the scoring multiples.

Play continues in rotation for as long as a player can lay a legitimate domino. It does not end if one player gets rid of all his dominoes, but only when no player can go. A player who does get rid of all his dominoes, however, scores an extra point for going out.

After each round, the first player is the one to the left of the previous first player. A running score is kept of all players' points, and the first to 41 is the winner.

What you will need A standard set of dominoes, pencil and paper to score

Example game

The illustration shows three hands, A, B, C, and how the game might develop. A goes first and lays 4, 5 for three points (the ends total 9). B lays 4, 1 for two points (the ends total 6). C lays 5, 2 for one point. A lays 2, 4 for one point. B lays the double-4 for three points. C lays the double-1 for two points. A lays the 4, 3 for one point. B lays the 1, 2 for one point. C lays 2, 3 for two points. A, on his turn now cannot go. B lays his double-3 for three points. C lays 3, 1, which doesn't score. This is the position in the game as laid out, with B on nine points, A and C on five. A can go now, and can score three points with 1, 6. And so on.

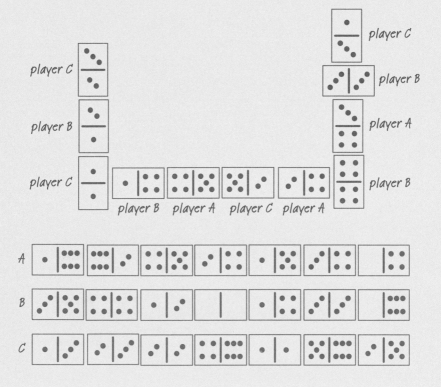

Bergen

Age range 8+
Number of players 2–4
Ideal for A group of dominoes enthusiasts looking for an interesting game

This is a fascinating game where points are scored in a way that doesn't apply to any other domino game – the object is simply to make both ends of the chain the same. But it is not always as simple as it looks.

How to play
From the shuffled face-down set, players take six dominoes each (if two or three players) or five each (if four players). The remaining dominoes form the bone yard.

The first player to play is the one holding the lowest double, discovered by asking 'Double-blank anyone?'. If nobody answers, ask for double-1 and so on. If there are no doubles out, the lowest domino is played.

The game follows the Block game (see page 158) and others previously described in that successive players must play to the chain in the centre a domino that matches one end of the chain. If a player cannot go, she must draw a domino from the bone yard. If this matches, she can play it, but if not she misses her turn, which passes to the player on the left. The last two dominoes in the bone yard are not drawn. A player who cannot go when there are only two dominos remaining in the bone yard misses her turn.

The object of the game is to score points by making both ends of the chain the same. If this is achieved with an ordinary domino (that is, not a double), you score two points for a 'double-header'. If it is achieved with a double, you score three points for a 'triple-header'.

The illustration of a game in progress explains this part of the scoring. Player A lays 1, 1 (the lowest double in play) and scores two points. B plays 1, 4 (no points), C plays 1, 6 (no points). D plays 6, 2 (no points). A plays 2, 4 (two points). B plays double-4 (three points). C plays 4, 5 (no points). D plays 5, 0 (no points). A plays 4, 3 (no points). B has to draw from the bone yard, gets 3, 6 and plays it (no points). C plays 0, 6 (two points). D plays double-6 (3 points) and so on.

Play continues until one player gets rid of all her dominoes and scores two points for doing so.

If play is blocked and nobody can go, the player with the lowest hand scores one point. The lowest hand is that which doesn't contain a double. If two or more hands are without a double, then that with the lowest total of spots wins – if tied, each get a point. If all hands contain a double, the point goes to the player with the least doubles – if tied, the player with the lowest double gets the point.

A running score is kept during successive games of the points scored by all players. With two players, the first to 15 points is the winner, with three or four players, the winner is the first to ten points.

What you will need A standard set of
dominoes, pencil and paper to score

Example game

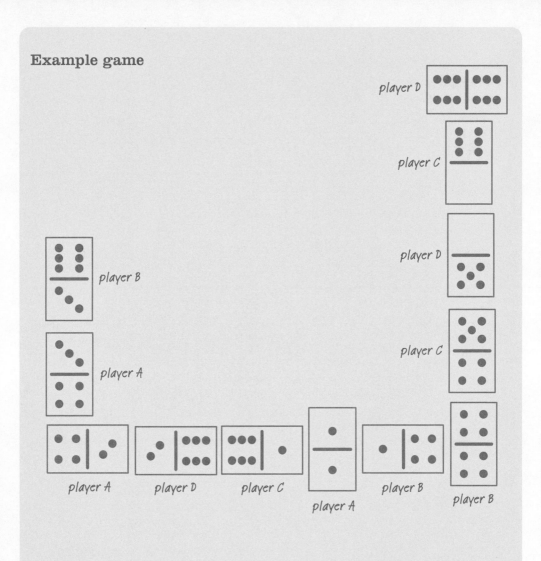

I went to the shops

Age range 10+
Number of players Any
Ideal for When a large party begins to get a bit boisterous

This is a game that can be played by all ages, but children younger than 12 might not have the memory to cope when the list gets long. If younger children want to join in, you could make it a teams-of-two game, pairing the youngsters with the adults so that they can prompt each other. The game should not be too serious.

How to play

The first player or team begins by saying 'I went to the shops and I came home with some apples'. The first player or team has to come home with something beginning with A, so apples would do. Artichokes or arsenic would have done as well.

The second player or team has to bring home something beginning with B, the first has to bring home something beginning with C, and so on through the alphabet. Where the difficulty lies is in the fact that each player or team has not only to provide something beginning with the appropriate letter, but has to repeat all the preceding articles as well.

Thus the second team could say 'I went to the shops and I came home with some apples and some bacon'. Bananas, bread or boots would fill the bill just as well, and in fact the game gets funnier if occasionally some outlandish goods are brought home: buffaloes, bongo-bongo drums, broomsticks or bunions.

The third team could say 'I went to the shops and I came home with some apples, some bacon and some candlesticks'.

It is when the sequence gets down to the Ps and Qs that people begin to crack, in more ways than one. Memorizing the list gets harder.

A player or a team who forgets an item on the list, or who cannot supply a new item for their letter, must drop out. The last player or team remaining is the winner, although if you successfully bring the list down to Z it might be as well to congratulate everybody still in on being mighty fine participants and turn to another game. This will be rare.

What you will need A good memory and a rosy nature (induced perhaps by the Christmas punch?), plus a working knowledge of alphabetical order

Variation

If you wanted to make the game harder, you could limit the goods to a narrow field (say flowers). For example, 'I went to the florists and came home with some asters… begonias… carnations… daisies…', but this could be seen as a touch serious. Suggested subjects might be:

Animals
Books (state the author)
CDs (state the name of the band)
Clothes
Fruit
Meat
Toiletries
Wine

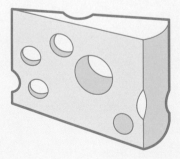

Buzz-fizz-raspberry

Age range 12+
Number of players Any
Ideal for Getting a party in silly mood
What you will need A sharp mind and a tolerant attitude to daft games

This is a game meant to be played fast and without anybody taking it too seriously. All ages can play, especially if they are sufficiently simple-minded.

How to play

Players sit in a circle, or at any rate positioned so that it is obvious whose turn is next.

The first player starts counting by calling 'One', the second counts 'Two' and so on for as long as it takes, except:

* When a number is divisible by three, the call is 'Buzz'.
* When a number is divisible by five, the call is 'Fizz'.
* When a number is divisible by seven, the player who has to call it blows a raspberry.

Some numbers will need a combination of these. Thus 15 will be 'Buzz-Fizz', 21 will be 'Buzz-Raspberry', and 35 will be 'Fizz-Raspberry'.

Any player who on his or her turn hesitates too long, or gets it wrong, is out and the sequence resumes with the following player.

The game keeps everyone alert, and causes amusement when people buzz instead of fizz, or if grandad has to blow a raspberry.

Age range 12+
Number of players Any up to 6
Ideal for Showing off your literacy at
an older party
What you will need A good vocabulary, a
dictionary to check spelling

A letter plus

This is a word game suitable for those who like to play their games sitting around, perhaps after a heavy meal.

How to play

Players sit in a circle. The player whose forename is first in the alphabet begins (an arbitrary rule). The first player chooses any three-letter word and begins by announcing its initial letter and a definition in the following manner: 'D plus two letters is not very bright.' He is thinking of the word dim. The definition must be accurate, and not cryptic or misleading.

Play proceeds to the left, so the second player, to the left of the first, must guess what the word is. If he is unsuccessful, he drops out of the game,

and the person to his left must try to identify the word. All players who make a wrong guess drop out. There may be arguments, which is part of the fun.

The player who identifies the word must think of a four-letter word beginning with D, and announce 'D plus three letters is a musical instrument of the percussion variety'. The next player to the left is first to try to identify the word, which of course is drum. The sequence could easily get to a ten-letter word or longer, so 'D plus nine letters is an explosion', the answer being detonation.

Eventually only one player is left and he or she is the winner. Then start a further round with another letter.

Cameras, cue, action

Age range 12+
Number of players Any up to 6
Ideal for Frustrated actors in the party

This is a game for all those who have sat in the theatre or cinema at a tense moment of drama in the action and thought, 'I could do that. I could be famous'. It is an alternative to the more traditional game of Charades, which sometimes becomes rather stereotyped.

Preparation

Draw up a list of adverbs, or alternatively if inspiration fails, spend a hard hour with a dictionary and find some. If it's many years since you were at school, an adverb is a word that modifies a verb, or put another way, describes how something is done. It nearly always ends in

'-y' and most probably in '-ly' (easily, happily, excitedly, disgracefully). When compiling this list, bear in mind that you are going to ask people to act the word, so choose only words that you can visualize being acted. It would be very disconcerting for somebody who was asked to act the word 'disingenuously', for instance. A dozen words are suggested here, with indications of how they might be acted.

How to play

A volunteer is required to start first. He or she is given the first word on your list and has to act the word. The other players have to guess what it is. There is a two-minute time limit (you will have to do the timing, which at least gets you out of the acting).

Variation

The audience can shout things to do in the style of adverb – the funnier the better. Try these:

'Eat a banana'
'Kiss your hand'
'Undo your shirt'
'Break dance'

What you will need A list of adverbs (see below) and, if you are going to play, nerve

If a player guesses correctly what the word is, he or she gets a point for cleverness and the actor gets a point for good acting. Players can keep their own scores. Ideally, everyone playing should have to do some acting, and when everybody has had a go, the player with most points is the winner. If it is a male, being an outstanding actor he can be called 'Oscar' for the rest of the evening. If it is a female, she can be called 'Renée Zellweger'.

The only words a participant is allowed to utter when acting are exclamations such as 'Wow', 'Oops', 'Crumbs' and 'Ouch'. On no account can they use words describing the adverb.

Some suggested adverbs

Quietly The actor can put his finger to his lips, say 'Sh' and tip-toe around.

Happily The actor smiles, laughs and dances around.

Clumsily The actor can pretend to bump into things, say 'Oops', and pretend to trip over his own feet.

Angrily The actor gnashes his teeth and tut-tuts.

Energetically The actor throws his arms around and generally bounces around.

Sadly The actor droops at the mouth and shoulders, cries and tries to look fed up.

Slowly The actor walks about in slow motion, blows his nose or scratches his ear very slowly.

Strongly The actor flexes his muscles and shows his biceps.

Flirtatiously The actor looks at a member of the opposite sex (preferably one he or she fancies), smiles, winks and makes any other gestures he or she thinks appropriate.

Accidentally The actor pretends to brush against something and knock it over, or bangs his head on something.

Drunkenly The actor reels about and simulates hiccups.

Hungrily The actor mimes eating very fast.

Ads, headlines, pictures

Age range 8+
Number of players Any (in teams)
Ideal for Parties for all the family, such as at Christmas

This is a game that the author has used often at Christmas, when it keeps people of all ages (above about eight or so) happily occupied for half-an-hour or more. They have to identify pictures, advertisements and news events cut from various papers and magazines.

Preparation

For a few weeks before the party, cut out from newspapers and magazines pictures of celebrities or events in the news, well-known advertisements and headlines to prominent stories.

With the pictures of people (they can be photos, but cartoons or caricatures are even more

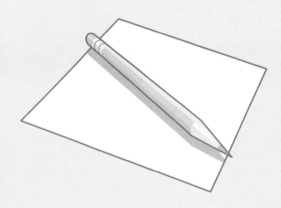

interesting), paste them without identities on sheets of A4 paper and number them, both the sheets and the pictures. Try to include pictures of people who younger people would recognize, such as pop stars. Keep a checklist of who they are. This is important – if you can't remember who they all are, there is no game! Pictures could be of an event in the news or a non-celebrity in the news – a multiple birth or a person convicted of murder – in which you might add a question under the picture, such as 'What news event was this?' or 'Why was this man in the news?'. With the advertisements, use well-known ones, but cut out the name of the company or product it is advertising. Paste those on sheets, number them and the sheets, and keep a checklist of answers.

With the headlines, remove a vital word and paste them on sheets, numbered as usual. Keep a checklist (you can actually paste the cut-out words on the answer sheet). At the end you should have about eight sheets, with an average of about ten items on each sheet to identify.

How to play

Divide the players into teams of three or four players. They do not need to be equal, so you can accommodate any number who wishes to play; four teams of four is very good. Mix up old and young in each team. Issue each team with sheets on which to write their answers and pens or pencils for them to write down their answers.

Give each team one of the question sheets, asking them to identify as many items as they can. They should write down, of course, the number of the sheet and the numbers of each item. As a team finishes with a sheet, replace it with a sheet they

What you will need A supply of
newspapers and magazines from which to
cut pictures and headlines, sheets on which
to paste them, glue, pencils and paper for
each team

haven't yet had. Harangue any team that takes too
long over one sheet – it is annoying if everybody
else has to wait at the end for a team with a
sheet or two still to see.

When everyone has finished, collect the question
sheets together and ask teams to swap their

answer sheets so that each team's answers are
checked by another team. Read out the answers.
There is often much surprise and calls of 'Let's
have another look' at some of the answers. The
team with most correct identifications is the
winning team.

Index

Acknowledgements

Executive Editor: Trevor Davies

Project Editor: Kate Tuckett

Executive Art Editor: Rozelle Bentheim

Designer: Mark Stevens

Illustrator: Peter Liddiard

Production Controller: Nigel Reed